How to Sew a Button

. . .

How to Sew a Button

And Other Nifty Things

Your Grandmother Knew

. . .

Erin Bried

Ballantine Books · New York

A Ballantine Books Trade Paperback Original

Copyright © 2009 by Erin Bried
Illustrations copyright © 2009 by Simon M. Sullivan

Published in the United States by Ballantine Books, an imprint of
The Random House Publishing Group, a division of
Random House, Inc., New York.

BALLANTINE and colophon are registered trademarks of
Random House, Inc.

LIBRARY OF CONGRESS CATALOGING-IN-PUBLICATION DATA

Bried, Erin.
How to sew a button: and other nifty things your grandmother
knew / Erin Bried.
p. cm.
ISBN 978-0-345-51875-0 (pbk.)
1. Home economics—Handbooks, manuals, etc.   2. Handicraft—
Handbooks, manuals, etc.   3. Life skills—Handbooks, manuals, etc.
I. Title.
TX145.B726 2009
640—dc22   2009036046

Printed in the United States of America

www.ballantinebooks.com

6 8 9 7 5

Book design by Simon M. Sullivan

To Noni, Grandma Shirley,

Mommom, Grandma Ro,

Grammy Lou, Grandma Sara,

and all grandmothers everywhere

Contents

. . .

3 · Cleaning

4 · Dressing

5 · Nesting

6 · Thriving

7 · Loving

8 · Saving

9 · Joining

10 · Entertaining

Introduction

...

More than a decade ago, I landed my dream job at Condé Nast, a world-renowned magazine publisher. On my first day of work, I arrived at the glamorous headquarters, then located on Madison Avenue, in my navy Payless pumps and my matching navy Casual Corner suit, which, for me, a twenty-two-year-old from semirural Pennsylvania, was high fashion. As a rover, or in-house temp, I filled in for the absent assistants of executives and senior editors of magazines, including *Vogue*, *GQ*, and *Glamour*. My first stop: the office of a certain big shot. When, with a trembling hand, I answered his phone for the first time, there was a woman with a thick Somalian accent on the other end. "This is Iman," she said. Throughout that day, I heard myself saying things like, "Princess Marie Chantal of Greece is on the line" and "A woman named Liz Smith asked that you call her. She didn't say where she was from." After lunch, my boss got a haircut by a stylist so famous he has his own line of shampoo. After work, he went to work out. I know this because I called my first-ever black car to take him to the gym. And so began my life in New York City.

Now, I'm the senior staff writer at *SELF* magazine, and my stories are read by more than six million women every month. I travel all over the country, sometimes even farther, to interview the celebrities who appear on our cover, and as a result, I've honed a very specific set of skills: namely, hailing cabs and ordering room service. At the photo shoots, where I spend many of my days watching the stars be photographed, there are always caterers, stylists, manicurists, even tailors, who are always happy to make a quick hem or repair any loose buttons. On the road, everything in life seems to be taken care of by other people.

And then I come home.

I recently invited some friends over for a dinner party, and for dessert I decided to do something extra special—make a strawberry-rhubarb pie. After searching for rhubarb high and low in just about every grocery store in Brooklyn, I was so happy and relieved when I finally found a bunch. It wasn't great-looking stuff—it was much thinner, redder, and leafier than I'd remembered it being—but it would do, I thought. You can't go wrong with pie. When I got it home, I followed the recipe carefully. I snipped off the leaves, chopped up the pencil-thin red stems, and tossed them into the pie with sugar, flour, and sliced berries. After I baked it to a perfect golden brown, I carried it to the table. My friends were so impressed. "Who makes pie these days?" they marveled. "I don't even know how to make a pie!" one confessed. I was so proud. Beaming, really. And then they each took a bite. That's when the compliments stopped. Silence. Crickets. A few sideways glances and lots of polite chewing-in-slow-motion. What a strange reaction to my delicious dessert, I thought. Then I tasted it, expecting a pink, sweet-tart sensation. Instead, I got a mouthful of green bitterness. It tasted like the smell of freshly cut grass. Mortified, I told my friends to stop eating. Clearly, I'd made a huge mistake. My enduring guests launched into a kindhearted interrogation, and together we discovered my error. It turns out that I'd accidentally bought Swiss chard instead of rhubarb, and I'd made the pie using the vegetable's stems, the part you normally throw away.

That's when it hit me: When I was a child, I used to help my grandmother clip rhubarb out of the garden; now, as an adult, I can't even identify the vegetable in the grocery store. Funny, yes, but also completely humiliating. When did I lose my ability to take care of myself?

The more I think about it, the less self-sufficient I realize I've become: It's been so long since I've done my own laundry that I can no longer remember if you wash colors in hot or cold. If I get pills on a sweater, I give it away. My breakfasts often come in bar form. My dinners usually come inside one of two things: a pizza box or a flour tortilla. I've killed more plants than I care to admit. And I've never once balanced my checkbook, much less devised a household budget.

What is simultaneously comforting and alarming about my domestic incompetence is that I am hardly alone. I'm joined by millions of women, Gen Xers and Gen Yers, who either have consciously rejected household endeavors in favor of career or, even more likely, were simply raised in the ultimate age of convenience and consumerism. Why do for ourselves, we shrug, when we can pay someone else to do it for us?

That's all begun to change.

We have now entered what experts are calling the worst economic crisis since the Great Depression. Suddenly, not knowing how to cook my own meals, care for my own house, iron my own shirts, even make my own entertainment (hello, cable!) seems not only disempowering, but also downright irresponsible. That's why I decided to do something about it. First step in moving forward: looking back.

My maternal grandfather died in 1956, leaving my late grandmother Hilda McFall to raise her two children alone. A feminist and activist, she soon became one of the first women elected to county office. As a Juilliard-educated pianist, she also supplemented her income by teaching lessons and playing in the theater. She kept her house immaculate, her beds made, her bathroom neat, and her lawn manicured. She always had a fresh pitcher of iced tea in the fridge and something delicious, like pasties or saffron buns, in the oven. She had close friends with whom she played cards into the night. Even though money was tight, she always managed to give each of her five grandchildren a crisp dollar at every visit and $50 every Christmas. She shopped locally and walked wherever she could, long before being green was a marketing concept. She was strong. She was prudent. And, above all, she was happy.

When I think about her life now, I'm truly awestruck, and I can think of no better role model for these tough times than our grandmothers, particularly those who survived the Great Depression. All grandmothers have stories about the clever, sometimes surprising, things they did to get by. They baked their own bread to save dough. They grew their own vegetables to feed their families. They wore their clothes well, until they wore them out. They took care of their neighbors and knew when to ask for help. They managed to keep romance alive without going out to fancy restaurants.

Since my own grandmothers are no longer alive, I reached out to others from all around the country to see what I could learn. (You can read more about them in the next section.) They told me stories about making do, helping others, finding fun, and even falling in love. As I was listening to each of them, I knew I was not only learning practical wisdom, like how to save money, live green, and take better care of myself and my family, but I was also collecting important stories, some of which have never been told before and all of which will soon disappear. Their stories are ones we need to remember.

If you are lucky enough to have your grandmother with you, sit and talk with her sometime. Ask her big questions, like what's the secret to a happy marriage, and little ones, like when was the first time she put on lipstick. Ask her nice questions, like what she did for fun, and cheeky questions, like if her father ever made whiskey in the basement (and if she ever snuck a taste). Ask her how she managed. Or just ask her to tell you a story, any story. I guarantee you'll be surprised by what you'll find out. If you no longer have your grandmother by your side, it's my hope that through this book, you'll now have the spirit of her next to you, offering you warm encouragement and gently guiding you through essential life tasks that you may have forgotten (or never even learned in the first place). I hope it will offer you calm, comfort, and, above all, confidence.

Meet the Grandmothers

• • •

It's my great pleasure to introduce you to these ten amazing grandmothers, all of whom have lived through the Great Depression and contributed their knowledge and stories to this book.

Elouise Bruce

Born on February 9, 1929, Bruce endured some hard times in the hills of Mississippi. She, along with her mother, father, and eight siblings, lived in a rented house on a Meridian farm, where cotton and corn was grown. While her father worked the land with a mule-drawn plow, Bruce and her siblings, from the age of eight onward, were expected to help support the family by picking cotton and delivering it to the gin, often even on school days. Despite their eleven-person-strong workforce, Bruce's family had no extra money. They grew what they ate, and ate everything fresh since they couldn't afford a refrigerator or often even a block of ice. She shared a twin bed with her three sisters. And they went barefoot when their shoes wore out. "Lord, I wouldn't want to go through it again," she says, still pained by her memories. Through perseverance and a good sense of humor, Bruce prevailed, marrying her sweetheart in 1940 and raising three children. She now lives with her husband in Cleveland, Mississippi, where she boasts of seven grandchildren (one of whom, she says, is even a nurse anesthetist) and five great-grandchildren.

Nikki Spanof Chrisanthon

Chrisanthon, the daughter of Greek immigrants, was born on February 5, 1925, and grew up in Allentown, Pennsylvania, where her father, an avid tap dancer, ran a candy and ice-cream shop. When the Depression hit, his business suffered, so her mother went to work in a dress factory. To make ends meet, Chrisanthon, along with her older sister, had to pitch in around the house by helping to buy groceries, cook, and clean. Despite the hard times, she still has fond memories of her childhood: having picnics in the park, seeing movies for a dime, and throwing grand parties with her relatives, which always included Greek dancing and singing. She lives with her husband of fifty-one years in Ocean City, New Jersey, where her three sons and six grandchildren visit her often.

Jean Dinsmore

Because her local hospital shut down due to the 1918 flu epidemic, Dinsmore was born at home on December 30 on her Troy, Idaho, farm. (She still has the old kerosene lamp that was burning the night she was born.) She learned to cook over her family's wood-fired stove at age ten, in order to help feed her father, two brothers, and the ten hired men who helped harvest the farm in the summer. By age twelve, she and her older sister moved alone to town, fifteen miles away from the farm, to get a proper education. Her mother always told her, "I don't care when you get married, but you have to finish college." Dinsmore did, and became a teacher before marrying "one of the neighbor boys" in 1940. The newlyweds moved to Spokane, Washington, where she still lives and regales her two children and five grandchildren with stories of the farm.

Grace Fortunato

Fortunato, the daughter of Italian immigrants, was born on July 29, 1930, in Brooklyn, New York, where she was also raised. After the Depression hit, her family moved into a two-bedroom apartment behind her father's barbershop, where her two brothers shared one room and she, her sister, and her parents shared the other. Every day, her father prepared traditional Italian meals (usually pasta and a vegetable, followed by fish) in their coal-fired oven. (Everything was made fresh because they lacked a refrigerator.) Fortunato, who stands five feet tall, weighs about one hundred pounds, and answers to "Honey," still makes some of her favorite family recipes in her Plantsville, Connecticut, kitchen for her husband of fifty-seven years, her five sons, and three grandchildren.

Lucile Frisbee

Frisbee was born on January 11, 1930, in idyllic Delhi, New York, where she still lives. Her father was the town pharmacist and her mother worked both in the pharmacy and as the town bookkeeper. Frugality and general belt-tightening helped the family ride out the Depression without suffering. She and her two sisters were accomplished musicians known about town as the Lee Trio. In fact, the girls would even take off from school to perform for local groups, including the Kiwanis Club and Eastern Star. When she wasn't practicing the piano, Frisbee remembers playing cards and stickball and spending hours assembling beautiful May baskets (flower bouquets, left in secret for a neighbor or loved one, on the first of May). She married a friend from high school in 1955, and when she's not helping him make and sell maple syrup, she shares her love of music with her three sons and five grandchildren.

Mildred Armstrong Kalish

Kalish was born on Saint Patrick's Day in 1922 and was raised on her grandparents' Iowa farm, which lacked both indoor plumbing and electricity. She spent many of her summer days befriending raccoons, taming colts, charming bees, and, of course, doing chores, like picking beans, loading hay, and gathering the cows for milking. After college and a brief stint in the Coast Guard, Kalish married, raised two sons, and became a professor of English at the University of Iowa, among other colleges. She now lives with her husband of sixty-five years in Cupertino, California, where she writes about her childhood. Her memoir, *Little Heathens* (Bantam), was named one of the ten best books of 2007 by the *New York Times Book Review*, which has surely made her four grandchildren and two great-grandchildren proud.

Alice Loft

Loft was born on August 26, 1921, in Centralia, Washington. Her father then worked for a lumber company, while her mother raised her and her four siblings. Loft spent much of her youth living on her grandparents' farm, where she learned to keep a garden, can produce, stoke the fire in a wood-burning stove, and gather eggs from the chicken coop. Her sponge cake, a direct result of collecting more eggs than she knew what to do with, once earned her a blue ribbon at the local fair. After she married, she had three kids and opened a gift shop that sold artisan crafts made from rare wood. In 1970, after her husband passed away, she went to work in her family's greenhouse. Now she lives with her cat, Callie, in Tacoma, Washington, where she still bakes delicious cakes for her seven grandchildren and three great-grandchildren.

Beatrice Neidorf

Born June 1, 1915, in Philadelphia, Neidorf was the youngest of three children. By the time the stock market crashed in 1929, she was attending school and working on weekends at one of the half dozen or so men's furnishing stores that her father owned. Though money was scarce, she enjoyed having connections in the clothing business. Her father was often able to procure some beautiful dresses for her, including one very memorable midnight-blue evening gown with a fringed back, which she wore to a dance. Because she knew her father couldn't afford to send her to college, Neidorf got a job at an auctioneer's office after graduating from high school. She worked there for nine years before meeting her husband, a pharmacist, and later moving to Washington, D.C. The two were happily married for fifty-two years. When she's not volunteering at the Kennedy Center, where she's donated her time for the past twenty-nine years, Neidorf bakes apple pies for her three daughters, four grandsons, and two great-grandchildren.

Sue Westheimer Ransohoff

Born on December 22, 1919, Ransohoff was nine years old when the stock market crashed. On October 29, 1929, she had plans to go trick-or-treating in her Baltimore neighborhood with her father, a stockbroker. "He didn't come home that night," she says. "I was too young to understand the implications. I just felt very let down." Because her father pulled most of his money from the market before the crash, her family remained relatively unscathed by the Depression, even as her neighbors were forced to leave their sizeable homes for smaller apartments. "For most of my life, I was embarrassed to be quite comfortable," she says. Still, having seen the fragility of wealth, Ransohoff, a graduate of Smith College, says she's been marked by the Depression. After losing her first husband in World War II and later marrying a former beau, she moved to Cincinnati, where she always both earned her own money (first as a social worker, and later as a writer and an art museum publicist) and helped those in need (as a volunteer for Planned Parenthood and the Hearing Speech and Deaf Center of Greater Cincinnati). She's known for throwing great parties, often attended by her four children, eight grandchildren, and one great-grandchild.

Ruth Rowen

The daughter of Russian immigrants, Rowen was born in New York City on April 19, 1914. She spent much of her childhood living in the only apartment building in the Bronx; the Bronx at that time was mostly pastoral farmland. When her mother fell ill, after giving birth to a younger brother, Rowen—twelve years old—took over running parts of the household. "That's when I grew up," she says, recalling her days of going to the market, returning to her mother's bedside, and asking her to "explain what had to be done with a chicken." Happily, her mother recovered, but Rowen never forgot the lessons she learned as a child during the Depression: Save money, make do, and be generous. In 1934, she married, and much to her in-laws' discontent, she started a career working at the New York Public Library. Now, still living in New York City, she shares her love of books with her daughter and granddaughter.

Cooking

. . .

*Cooking at home is cheaper, healthier,
and just plain better.*

Wake Up Happy

• • •

"I do think anyone who can read can learn to cook."
—MILDRED KALISH

HOW TO MAKE BLUEBERRY PANCAKES

Step 1: If you've got the blueberries, chances are you've also got everything else you need to make these tasty flapjacks for two. Gather your ingredients: 1 egg (beaten but not conquered), 1 cup milk, 2 tablespoons canola oil (or melted butter), 1 tablespoon sugar, 1¼ cups flour, ½ teaspoon salt, 3 teaspoons baking powder, and ¾ cup blueberries (fresh or frozen).

Step 2: Did that take you forever? If so, chug a cup of joe. Then, in a large bowl, using an electric or hand beater, mix your egg, milk, oil, and sugar.

Step 3: With a wooden spoon, stir in the flour, salt, and baking powder. Don't stress about the lumps! It's better to leave a few in.

Step 4: Pop a few blueberries in your mouth, and then add the rest to the batter.

Step 5: Add a pat of butter (or a drizzle of oil) to a frying pan, and bring it to a sizzle on medium heat. No matter how hungry you are, resist turning up the flame or you'll have burned pancakes with raw insides.

Step 6: Using a ladle, drop some batter into the center of the pan to form a flapjack of your desired size. A quarter-cup drop will yield about nine palm-sized cakes.

Step 7: When the edges begin to bubble up, scoot a spatula beneath the flapjack and flip it over. Refrain from throwing it in the air, unless your floor is super clean and no one is watching.

Step 8: Once both sides are golden brown, remove from heat, plate, and serve.

More Nifty Tips

- If you're going to use frozen berries, defrost them first.
- Spritz a few drops of water into your frying pan before adding the batter. If it sizzles, you'll know it's ready. If not, keep it on the fire a little longer.
- Serve with real maple syrup if you've got it!

Be a Strong Chick

...

"Chicken was a special dinner, because we didn't buy any meat back then. We'd just get one from out back, wring his head off, cook him, and eat him. I didn't dread doing it then, but I wouldn't want to do it now."
—ELOUISE BRUCE

HOW TO ROAST A WHOLE CHICKEN

Step 1: Go to your local butcher, farm, or grocer and buy the whole bird. You'll need about ¾ pound per person. Dig out your roasting pan, and crank up your oven to 375 degrees. Then, shush! Give a listen. Is your belly growling? If so, have a little snack. It takes a good hour to roast a 3- to 3½-pound bird.

Step 2: Get acquainted with your chicken. If you're temporarily grossed out, there's no kind way to say this: Get over yourself. You're about to eat this bird (and it's going to be delicious), so you might as well take responsibility for cooking it. Then, peek inside your chicken. If you see a bag of parts, pull it out. (It's the giblets, or heart, neck, and liver of *a* chicken, not necessarily *your* chicken. You can simmer them in water to make a broth or gravy, or you can just toss them.)

Step 3: Give your bird a bath for good measure. Rinse it, inside and out, under cold water, and then pat it dry with a paper towel.

Step 4: Prepare your seasonings. Mix softened butter (about ½ to ¾ stick) with generous amounts of your favorite herbs and spices.

Try chopped garlic (4 to 6 cloves), diced rosemary (about 5 full twigs' worth), and salt and pepper (½ teaspoon or more). Or, chopped garlic, lemon zest, thyme, and tarragon. How much of each? Enough. Basically, just throw it all together. It's hard to cluck it up.

Step 5: Using your fingers (or, if you're still grossed out, an upside-down spoon), separate the skin from the meat, being careful not to rip or puncture it, or your bird will lose its juices. Once you've got some wiggle room in there, smush your butter mixture between the skin and meat, making sure to get it into every nook and cranny. Then, rub butter all over the outside of the bird, too, so it'll brown nicely in the oven.

Step 6: Season the inside of your chicken. Sprinkle in a good amount of salt and pepper, and then toss in a couple of whole garlic cloves, whatever leftover herbs you might have from your butter mixture (stems included), and a quartered lemon.

Step 7: Place your bird, breast and legs up, in your roasting pan. Tuck the tip of the wings underneath the body and, if you'd like, tie the legs together with kitchen string. It's not necessary, but it adds a dose of fancy.

Step 8: Pop your chicken in the oven, set your timer for an hour, go have a glass of wine or a gimlet, and wait.

Step 9: When the timer goes off, check on your chicken. Tilt it until some juices run out. If they're pinkish, it's not done yet. If they're clear, stick a kitchen thermometer into the fattest part of the thigh. Only when it reads 165 degrees is it done.

Step 10: Set your chicken on a platter on the countertop and let it rest for 10 minutes, so it gets good and juicy. (If you'd like to make gravy, now's the time. See page 8 for instructions.)

Step 11: Present your chicken to your dinner guests, preferably using grand gestures. Enjoy their *ooh*s and *aah*s, and then enjoy the chicken.

More Nifty Tips

• Buy an organic bird, if you can. That means it was raised with outdoor access and without antibiotics and was fed a vegetarian organic diet. It'll taste better and give you good karma.

• When buying a fresh chicken, check the sell by date before purchasing and eyeball the amount of juice in the package. Lots of liquid may mean the bird has been sitting around for a while.

• To defrost a frozen chicken, keep it wrapped, put it on a tray, and set it in your fridge 24 hours before you plan to roast it. Do *not* set it out on your countertop, or you'll have some serious bacteria issues.

• No roasting pan? Buy a cheapo aluminum one and set it on a cookie tray (for stability) before placing it in the oven.

• For a healthier option, skip the butter. Just rub your bird with dry herbs and spices, and then drizzle with olive oil. Mmmmm.

• Always wash your hands—hello—*with* soap, after handling raw chicken.

• After you eat the chicken, toss the carcass in a large pot and cover with water. Add a few whole onions, some carrot chunks, and quartered celery stalks, plus salt and pepper. Bring to a boil, then let simmer for 4 hours. Skim off the fat, transfer to airtight containers, and store in the freezer for up to 3 months. Homemade chicken stock tastes better than anything you can get in a store, and it's cheaper, too!

Get Sauced

. . .

"Gravy was always on our table. It was just part of the meal. A potato wasn't anything without gravy. It's so good."
—ALICE LOFT

HOW TO MAKE GRAVY

Step 1: While your just-out-of-the-oven meat rests on your serving platter for 10 minutes, pour the drippings from the roasting pan into a bowl. Then, have a glass of wine while you wait for the fat to float to the top. It'll take a few minutes.

Step 2: Gently spoon off the fat, or the top layer of clear goop, so your gravy isn't a greasy mess. Transfer whatever's left in your bowl back to the pan.

Step 3: Set your roasting pan directly on a burner, fired up to medium heat. Add 1 cup stock and, with a wooden spoon, scrape the bottom of the pan to free up any yummy bits. Let simmer.

Step 4: In a separate bowl, make a thickener by mixing 2 tablespoons flour with 4 tablespoons stock. Whisk it like crazy until all lumps are gone.

Step 5: Pour your thickener into your roasting pan, and whisk like you've never whisked before. Keep going until your gravy (and your bicep) is sizzlingly hot and as thick as you'd like. Too thick? Add more stock. Too thin? Whip up some more flour paste (one part flour to two parts stock) and add. Too stressed? Have another glass of wine.

Step 6: Season your gravy with salt and pepper, and pour it into a fancy boat or old chipped bowl. Doesn't matter what you put it in, it's still going to taste divine. Serve.

More Nifty Tips

- For creamier gravy, replace half the stock with milk.

- To stretch your gravy, just add more stock in step 3 and make more thickener (one part flour to two parts stock) in step 4.

- If you're having trouble skimming the fat off the drippings (step 2), pop the drippings in the freezer for a few minutes. The fat will glob up on top, which makes it easier to scoop out.

Talk Turkey

· · ·

"The people who love to eat make the best cooks."
—Grace Fortunato

How to Carve a Roasted Bird

Step 1: Choose your longest, most impressive-looking knife, and hone it. (See page 27 for instructions.) The sharper your blade, the less likely it'll appear that a caveman cooked your Thanksgiving dinner.

Step 2: Position the turkey, breast side up, drumsticks pointing toward you, and snip off any strings.

Step 3: Remove the legs. With your knife along the body, blade down, slice through the skin that attaches the leg to the body, down along the thigh meat, and finally through the joint, where the bones meet. (Don't saw through any bones, Hannibal. You'll make a mess. Just use the tip of your knife to sever the joint.) Set the leg and thigh aside, and repeat once more unless you bought a one-legged bird. (If you did that, hopefully you got a discount.)

Step 4: Poke that crazy-long, two-pronged fork that you've probably never used and that came with your knife set into the wing to secure the bird, and then turn your knife blade parallel to your work surface. Make a horizontal cut into the bird, just above the wing and below the breast.

Step 5: Poke your fork into the top of the bird, place your knife halfway up the breast, and slice down until you meet your horizontal cut. Place that piece of meat on a serving platter, and repeat, working your way up the breast to carve thin slices.

More Nifty Tips

- Let your bird rest for 10 to 15 minutes before carving to seal in the juices.

- Sneak a folded paper towel between the turkey and the plate. It'll keep the turkey from sliding around.

- Separate the drumsticks from the thighs before serving to prevent fights at your table.

- Trim off the wings, if anyone would like those, at their joints with poultry shears.

- Save your carcass to make a stock. See page 7 for tips.

- If you have any questions while carving, and your grandmother isn't around to call, try the Butterball Turkey Hotline at 1-800-BUTTERBALL. Seriously. It's open weekdays from 10 A.M. to 7 P.M. (CST), and operators will answer all your birdbrained questions for free.

Be a Good Catch

. . .

"You just can't go fishing, and expect somebody else to clean your catch."
—Nikki Spanof Chrisanthon

How to Fillet a Fish

Step 1: If you're at all squeamish, take a deep breath, and know this: The fish is already a goner, and it's not nearly as slimy as you think it's going to be.

Step 2: Lay your fish flat on a cutting board, belly facing away from you, give thanks, and then grab your thinnest, sharpest, longest knife.

Step 3: Lifting up the pectoral fin (the little one behind the gills), place your knife, blade down, perpendicular to the fish, make your most dramatic grimace, and cut downward to (but not through) the backbone. Whew! That's over with. Nice job.

Step 4: Starting behind the head and using just the tip of your knife, run your blade along the top edge of the fish, near the dorsal fin, to the tail, slicing along (but not through) the rib cage. As the meat separates from the fish, peel it back and repeat your gentle slicing from head to tail until the full fillet is free. See? That wasn't so bad at all.

Step 5: Flip the fish, and repeat steps 2 through 4, for the second fillet. Now, you're a total pro—and you're almost finished!

Step 6: Inspect each fillet carefully. If you see any bones, pluck them out. Once you think you've got them all out, run your fingers over your fillet to double-check, or your meal may be more memorable—cough, cough—than you bargained for.

Step 7: Remove the skin by placing each fillet, skin side down, on the cutting board. Holding your knife blade at a 45-degree angle, start on one end and cut through the meat down to (but not through) the skin. Then, pressing the loosened skin down with your fingernail to secure it, turn your blade parallel to your work surface and gently work it down the length of the fillet. Go easy now. Don't force it.

Step 8: Rinse the fillets with cold water, and fry 'em up!

More Nifty Tips

- If you're buying, not catching, your fish, peek inside the gills. If they're red, it's fresh.

- Too slimy? You can always wear a pair of gloves.

- Squeeze lemon juice on your hands after filleting and before washing to help your patties smell fresh.

Rise Up and Save Dough

. . .

"I remember Mother baking bread. That sure smelled good when you walked home from school. I loved getting a slice with butter. My sister and I each liked the heels. She'd have a hand on one end and I'd have a hand on the other, but my mother put a stop to that."
—JEAN DINSMORE

HOW TO BAKE BREAD

Step 1: Gather up your ingredients: 3 cups bread flour, 3 cups whole wheat flour, 3¾ cups tepid water, 2½ teaspoons salt, and 1¼ teaspoons instant dry yeast (aka "RapidRise yeast"). You'll also need two loaf pans, a touch of oil or butter, and the patience of Job. It's best if you set yourself up with something productive to do, besides clicking "refresh" on your Facebook page for hours.

Step 2: In a large bowl, dump in all your ingredients, and combine them into a shaggy mass using your hands. You'll know you've done it right if your mixture looks like a bad '70s carpet. Don't be afraid to get messy!

Step 3: Wash and dry your hands, then roll up your sleeves. You're getting ready to knead some dough.

Step 4: Lightly dust your clean countertop with your bread flour (not too much!). Scrape the dough out of the bowl onto the countertop, using a spatula or a plastic scraper. Then, get a wee bit of flour on your hands.

Step 5: Knead that dough, baby. To do so, fold the top portion of the dough toward you and, with the heel of your hand, gently press the dough away from you. Turn the dough a quarter turn, and repeat until the dough begins to get smooth. Be patient; this could take several minutes. The more you knead the dough, the lighter and fluffier your bread will be. If and when it begins to stick to your hands or the countertop, stop kneading and scrape it up and redust your countertop with flour. Also, unmuck your hands by rubbing them together vigorously; then put a little more flour on them, too.

Step 6: Now comes the really fun part: throwing the dough. Using both hands, pick up the dough by the edge closest to you. Make sure nobody is standing behind you, then swing it back over your shoulder and fling it onto the counter. You'll know you've done it correctly if the dough stretches long and makes a ridiculously satisfying slapping sound upon contact. Then, fold the top down and turn it by a quarter. Gleefully, repeat the entire sequence—throw, fold, turn—for several minutes until the dough is smooth and elastic and you're strangely flushed. To test its readiness, tug on it. It should feel resistant and shouldn't break easily.

Step 7: Grease a clean large bowl with a tiny bit of butter or oil, toss in your dough, and flip it a few times so all the sides are coated. Place plastic wrap (nothing else will do) over the top of your bowl and set a timer for 1 hour. Go relax while the yeast gets busy.

Step 8: Revisit your dough when your timer goes off. It may not have risen very much yet at all, but fear not. It will. Remove the plastic wrap and picture your dough as a square. Using two hands, grab one side of the "square," give it a little stretch, fold it to the center, and pat it down. Turn your bowl by a quarter, and repeat on the remaining three sides. Flip your dough over so that the smooth side is up, replace your plastic wrap, and set your timer for 1 more hour. Go chill out again.

Step 9: Time to divide the dough. Dust your countertop with flour. Using your scraper or spatula, loosen the dough from your bowl and flip it out onto the flour. Cut the dough in half, using a scraper or knife, and pick up both pieces to make sure they feel equal in weight.

Step 10: Roughly round each piece of dough by gathering up the edges to the middle as if you were forming a pouch from a piece of cloth. Flip the dough over and tuck the edges under to loosely finish the ball. Leaving your dough on the countertop, cover it with plastic wrap, and set your timer for 15 minutes. In the meantime, grease two standard loaf pans (9" x 5") with softened butter or oil, making sure to get all the corners and edges.

Step 11: Shape your dough into something that looks like a loaf of bread. Dust a little flour on top of the dough and countertop. Using the scraper, loosen the dough from the counter and flip it over onto the flour, so the bottom is facing up. Gently tug two ends of the dough to form a rectangle with the short ends facing you. Fold in the long sides just a wee bit, and then gently pat it down. Grab the bottom short side of the dough with both hands and fold it into the center, sealing it with several taps of the heel of one hand. Repeat with the top edge of the dough. Next, place your fingers under the top of the dough and fold the top edge three-quarters of the way down the loaf. Press the seam down with your fingertips. Placing your thumbs on the seam you just created, fold the top of the dough down once more to meet the bottom edge. Tap the seam with the heel of your hand. Flip the dough, seam side down, and if it's not long enough, roll it gently with the palms of your hands until it's the length of the pan. Place the dough in the pan, seam-side down, and repeat with the remaining dough. Cover with plastic wrap, set your timer for another hour, and preheat your oven to 450 degrees. Now you're getting close!

Step 12: Check your dough to see if it's ready to bake. It should have risen just over the top of the pan and be light and springy to the touch. If it isn't yet ready, go mope a little bit while you let it rise for another 30 minutes or so. If it is ready, pop it in the oven, spacing the pans evenly, and set a timer for 20 minutes.

Step 13: Once your bread has been baking for 20 minutes, check on it. Rotate your pans, and check the color of your bread. It should just be turning a light golden brown. If it's getting darker than you'd like, turn down your oven to 400 degrees. Regardless, bake for another 12 to 15 minutes.

Step 14: Remove your golden-brown bread from the oven and flip it out of the pan. Knock on the bottom of each loaf. If it sounds hollow, your bread is finished! Transfer to a cooling rack.

Step 15: Now, a test of will: Before slicing into your bread, you must wait at least an hour for the dough to set and the carbon dioxide inside it to dissipate. For now, enjoy the smell and start planning what you'd like to spread on top of it. You can never go wrong with butter!

More Nifty Tips

- Measure your yeast or salt over the sink, not your bowl, so you don't accidentally add too much.

- Don't stress. Kneading takes a little practice, but you'll find your rhythm soon enough. Besides, bread dough is forgiving, so you'll have something good to eat no matter what.

- If you'd like sweeter bread, add 1 cup nuts or dried fruit (or any combination thereof) between steps 6 and 7. Just flatten your dough on the counter, sprinkle in your fixings, and knead several times.

- Keep opened yeast in the fridge and whole wheat flour in the freezer to maintain freshness. White bread flour can be stored in a cabinet.

- If you have a pizza stone, place it on the middle rack of your oven while your oven preheats. Baking your loaves on top of the stone (in pans) will make your bread lighter.

- To keep bread fresh, store at room temperature or wrap it in plastic and freeze it for up to 3 months. To thaw, keep it wrapped and set it out for several hours or unwrap it and put it in a 425-degree oven for 5 minutes.

Find a Slice of Heaven

. . .

"People are afraid of pie crusts, but they're not hard to make. And good filling makes all the difference."
— Beatrice Neidorf

How to Make a Pie

Step 1: Preheat your oven to 425 degrees, and make some dough for the crust. Dump 2 cups flour and 1 teaspoon salt in a large bowl. Add ⅔ cup plus 2 tablespoons Crisco, and crisscross your mixture with two butter knives until you've got pea-sized crumbles. Sprinkle in 1 tablespoon ice water and toss with a fork. Add 4 or 5 more tablespoons water, one at a time, and toss until your dough sticks together. Don't mush it around too much, or it'll get tough.

Step 2: Gather your dough into two balls (heh), cover with plastic wrap, flatten into disks, and place in refrigerator until chilled, at least 45 minutes.

Step 3: In the meantime, make your filling in a large bowl.

For an apple pie: Peel, core, and slice 8 or so large apples, and stir in ⅓ cup sugar, ¼ cup flour, ½ teaspoon each cinnamon and nutmeg, and a dash of salt.

For a berry pie: Stir together 6 cups of berries with ¾ cup sugar, ½ cup flour, and the juice of 1 lemon.

For a strawberry-rhubarb pie: Stir together 3 cups chopped rhubarb (make sure it's not Swiss chard!), 3 cups strawberries, 2 cups sugar, ⅔ cup flour, and the zest of 1 orange.

Step 4: Generously dust your clean countertop with flour, plunk the dough in the center, and, with a well-floured rolling pin, roll out the dough from the center to form a circle about 4 inches larger in diameter than your pie plate. Lift and turn the dough every few rolls to keep it even and to prevent it from sticking to your surface.

Step 5: Transfer the dough to your pie plate. This is the toughest part, but know that if you rip your dough, it's easy to fix it, so the pressure's off! Feeling good and loose? Okay, then. Gently fold your dough in half, and then into quarters, scoop it up with a spatula, set it in your pie plate, and unfold it. Step back and admire your handiwork. Say ta-da!

Step 6: Fill the pie with whatever goodness you've concocted, and place dabs of butter all over the top of it.

Step 7: Roll out your upper crust in the same way. Then moisten the edges of your bottom crust with water or milk, and lay the top crust over your pie.

Step 8: With a pair of scissors or a knife, trim the excess dough from both crusts, leaving about 1 inch on all sides.

Step 9: Curl both edges under together and tuck them into the pie plate. Then crimp them, by pinching the dough between the knuckle of your right index finger and the thumb and forefinger of your left hand. Once you make it all the way around the pie and it looks great, say ta-da again, this time with feeling!

Step 10: With a sharp knife, cut four tiny holes in the center of the upper crust, so the steam can escape. If you make the chimneys teardrop shaped, everyone will be impressed. Then paint the crust with milk, so it'll bake up golden brown.

Step 11: Carefully place your pie in the oven and bake for 40 to 45 minutes. (Strawberry-rhubarb pie takes 55 minutes.) Once it's golden brown, remove it from the oven and let it cool on a wire rack for as long as your self-restraint allows. Then present it with a big "Ta!" and then a "Da!"

More Nifty Tips

- If you're worried about your crust sticking to your work surface, roll it out between two sheets of waxed paper.

- Heal any tears by affixing some spare dough with a few drops of water or milk.

- Wrap aluminum foil around the edges of the crust before baking (or use a pie shield) to prevent them from burning. Remove it 10 minutes before baking is finished.

- To prevent the bottom crust from getting soggy, paint it with a beaten egg white before filling.

- No Crisco? Use butter in the crust. It'll still be oh so flavorful, just a little less flakey.

- Don't toss your leftover dough. Gather it into a ball, roll it out, sprinkle with cinnamon and sugar, slice into pinwheels (or whatever your heart's delight), and bake. Mmm, pie appetizers!

Drink to Your Health

. . .

"We prided ourselves on our economy.
You never threw anything away."
—RUTH ROWEN

HOW TO MAKE A SMOOTHIE
WITH FRUIT OR VEGGIES

Step 1: Peek in your fridge, and grab any fruits or veggies that look like they need to be eaten immediately or will go to waste. Check your garden, too, in case you've got any produce that has just barely overripened on the vine.

Step 2: Choose your flavor. Apples and pears can sweeten up carrots, spinach, celery, and parsley. Tomatoes and cucumbers pair off well. Generally all fruits go nicely with each other. And, mmm! Mint complements melon smoothies like nobody's business.

Step 3: Peel and finely chop up whatever you've got. Toss your finds into a blender.

Step 4: Add some apple or orange juice, and puree. Repeat, until you reach the desired consistency.

Step 5: Add 2 to 4 ice cubes, and blend to crush.

Step 6: Take a sip to check the flavor, and season if you'd like. To sweeten fruity smoothies, add honey. To spice up savory juices, add hot pepper, Worcestershire sauce, a squeeze of lemon, and salt and pepper.

More Nifty Tips

- For fruity drinks, substitute frozen berries for ice cubes.

- For creamier smoothies, add a scoop of yogurt.

- Even if your drink turns out green and reminds you of pond scum, close your eyes and bottoms up! It'll be chock-full of vities and make you feel strong.

Save Your Bacon

. . .

"We cooked breakfast at 6 A.M. on the farm. We had ten hired men during harvest, so we'd have eggs and bacon and all that good heavy stuff. Had to fill up all those men!"
—JEAN DINSMORE

HOW TO USE GREASE AS FLAVORING

Step 1: Fry up some bacon, and have it for breakfast. It is arguably the most indulgent way to start your day—even more so if you can get someone else to fry it for you! (To accomplish that, open this book to pages 194–195 and leave it in a conspicuous spot for your honey to find.)

Step 2: After you eat but before the grease sets, pour the warm (not sizzling-hot) bacon drippings through a mesh strainer into a glass jelly jar or well-washed coffee can, and store in the fridge or freezer.

Step 3: Reach for your stash, and use it instead of butter or shortening, to add flavor to savory dishes, like scrambled eggs or fried potatoes, beans or biscuits.

More Nifty Tips

- No strainer? Lay a paper towel over your container, and pour the grease through that.

- Use bacon grease only in moderation to keep your ticker healthy.

- Don't pour hot grease into a cold glass jar, or it could shatter. Wait for the grease to cool a bit before transferring it. (If you're pouring it into metal, do it at any time.)

Stay Sharp

. . .

"The knife sharpener came around with a horse and a wagon. We'd hear him, and you'd go out with whichever knives needed sharpening. It cost next to nothing."

— Grace Fortunato

How to Hone a Knife

Step 1: With a dry towel, wipe the steel. That's the long, rough rod that came with your knife set. You've been wondering what it was for, right? Well, today is your lucky day. You're about to find out.

Step 2: Gripping its handle with your weaker hand, place the steel, point-down, on your countertop or other flat surface. Hold it still.

Step 3: Grip the knife in your dominant hand, holding it the same way you would if you were about to cut a tomato (that is, parallel to your work surface, sharp side down, point away from you). Keeping the knife in that same position, place the sharp edge of the blade (nearest to the knife's handle) flat against the top of the steel (just below its handle). Now, rotate your knife-holding hand by one-eighth of a turn (clockwise, if you're right-handed; counterclockwise if you're left-handed), so the sharp side of your knife meets the steel at an approximately 20-degree angle. (The sharp edge of your knife should still be facing downward.) Hopefully, you've heard this before, but it's worth saying again: Never, ever point a sharp knife toward yourself.

Step 4: While pulling your knife toward you and maintaining your 20-degree angle, slide the sharp side of your blade from the top of the steel toward the bottom. You'll know you've done the motion correctly if it ends with the tip of your knife coming off the bottom of the steel.

Step 5: Switch sides, and repeat. Just place your knife on the opposite side of the steel, again just below the handle. Find that same 20-degree angle by rotating your knife-holding hand by an eighth of a turn (counterclockwise, if you're right-handed; clockwise if you're left-handed) and swipe.

Step 6: Repeat steps 4 and 5 four more times.

Step 7: Wipe your blade with a towel to remove shavings and test its sharpness by slicing into the edge of a piece of paper. If it cuts it easily, then it's ready to use. If not, repeat step 6 and test again.

Step 8: Count your fingers. All there? Then it was a success!

More Nifty Tips

- Another way to find an angle close to 20 degrees: Hold your blade perpendicular to your steel. That's 90 degrees. Tilt your blade (sharp side facing down more) to cut that angle in half (45 degrees). Repeat once more to find 22.5 degrees.

- Don't sweat the angle too much. Anything less than 45 degrees will do, so long as you stay consistent.

- Sharpen your knife before every use to make slicing and dicing easier (and safer).

- If your knife is huge, congrats! Slide your grip up from the handle a bit until only the fleshy part of your thumb rests on the handle and your fingers are gripping the dull sides of the blade. That'll give you a little more control.

- Take it slow! The speed at which you hone has no bearing on the results.

Fill Your Plate

. . .

"You knew what you were going to eat, depending on what was on sale."
—Ruth Rowen

How to Plan a Week's Menu

Step 1: Don't stress. Breakfast is easy to plot. Lunch is no big whup. And planning your dinners in advance will save you from running to the store after a long day at work and shopping when you're so hungry you can't think straight. Take a piece of paper (don't eat it!) and write down each day of the week across the top.

Step 2: Check your calendar for the week. On busy days, plan for easy dinners, like pasta. On lazy days, try something more adventurous. Make a note of it on your schedule.

Step 3: Check your kitchen. Peek inside your fridge and pantry to see if you've got any ingredients that must be used right away. Walk out to your garden, if you have one, to see what's ripe.

Step 4: Consider the season. If you don't have your own garden, remember that freshly harvested produce tastes better, costs less, and helps support your local farms (and the environment). And honestly, can you imagine anything better than locally grown heirloom tomatoes in the summertime? Add any seasonal produce to your shopping list.

Step 5: Check for sales. Skim the newspaper for coupons and store circulars, and plan your meals around them. If chicken is cheap this week, include it in a dinner or two. If beef is on sale, consider a burger or steak night.

Step 6: Given all that you know, write down your seven dinner ideas. If you need ideas, flip through your cookbooks, look online, or call a friend for her favorite recipe.

Step 7: Break down each meal into ingredients, and add them to your shopping list.

Step 8: Hit the store, and feel good knowing you're saving yourself time and money!

More Nifty Tips

- Not sure what's in season in your area? Go to PickYourOwn .org.

- Make your menu on a full belly, and you'll be less likely to plan for things like "Dorito night" or "Pasta in a bread bowl" dinner.

- Your dinners should hover around 500 calories, so don't feel pressured to make extravagant meals every night. Lighter bites will do.

- Try to use as many whole foods as possible. If it doesn't come off a tree or out of the ground, it's probably not good for you.

- Make every plate a rainbow. The more (naturally) colorful your meal, the more likely you are to be getting your vitamins.

2

Gardening

...

*Food prices are rising and food safety is sketchy,
but produce from your garden is organic and free.
Nothing is more local than your own backyard.*

Grow Your Own

. . .

"There was an incredible pleasure in going out to the garden with a dish pan and paring knife to pick beans."
—MILDRED KALISH

HOW TO PLANT A VEGETABLE GARDEN

Step 1: Choose a spot. Anywhere with loads of sunshine (at least six hours a day) and good drainage will do, whether it's a backyard plot, a raised rooftop container, a window box, or simply a single pot. A garden is a garden, no matter the size. Take pride in yours.

Step 2: Plan your crop. Based on your climate, your time, your tools, and your taste buds, choose which vegetables you'd like to grow, and purchase the seeds from your local garden or hardware store. Don't be afraid to ask your neighbor or local farmer for advice. And remember, you'll get much more out of a smaller, well-kept garden than a larger, unmanageable patch, so be honest with yourself about what you can swing.

Step 3: Prepare the soil. Using a shovel, dig your garden seven to ten inches deep. Turn the soil until it's soft and fluffy, working out any clumps, grass, rocks, or weeds. Don't be afraid to work up a sweat. With glistening skin and little smudges of dirt on your cheeks, you'll look hot (in a good way). Mix in any compost (see page 43) if you have it.

Step 4: Sow your seeds according to the instructions on the back of the seed packets. Depth (often just a finger poke) and spacing (usually six to twelve inches) are key for healthy plants. Label each row with a wooden stake (or even just a popsicle stick), marked with the name of the crop.

Step 5: Water your garden once a week (it needs about an inch of H_2O) in the early morning (before the temperatures begin to rise), and watch it grow!

More Nifty Tips

- Don't forget to wear a hat and sunscreen when you're working, even on cloudy days.

- Pull weeds (root and all) regularly. Unlike punk-rock hair, wild gardens don't rock. If they're unkempt, your veggies will be sapped of nutrients, light, and water.

- To learn more about gardening, visit garden.org.

Keep Away Pests

• • •

"You had to have a garden. You had no alternative. I can remember
crawling on my hands and knees down the line to thin out the carrots.
That was a hard chore, but I had a good time doing it. You sure would be
happy when you got through."
—Jean Dinsmore

How to Naturally Protect Your Garden from No-Good Insects

Step 1: Plant wisely. Select crops that will thrive in your area. The
stronger and healthier your plants are, the better they'll be able to
withstand pests. Also, move your crops around each year. Insects
can be lazy bastards, so if you move their favorite foods even just a
few feet away, they may not make the effort to follow them. Keep in
mind, though, that they're not picky eaters, either. They'll eat any
veggie within the same family, so don't swap, say, green beans for
wax beans or broccoli for cauliflower. Really mix things up.

Step 2: Run interference. Plant marigolds, tansy, thyme, dill,
lemon balm, or garlic (or *any* unrelated flowers or veggies) between
each crop. Your barrier plants will not only discourage insects from
chomping down the entire row, but they also may attract good-for-
your-garden ladybugs, who will eat your greedy guests.

Step 3: Visit your garden daily, and give it a good once-over. If
you see any hungry insects wreaking havoc on your crops, take a
deep breath and then send them to la-la land. Squish them, stomp

on them, or drop them in a bucket of soapy water. It sounds rather grim, and possibly even a bit mean, but remember, it's your responsibility to feed your family, not uninvited pests. You are the quickest, most effective, most natural pesticide available.

Step 4: Set traps. Leave a rolled-up newspaper near your garden to collect earwigs, and a board on the ground to collect slugs. (No board? Slugs, those slimy little lushes, will also dive into a lidful of beer.) Check your traps once a day and sprinkle any suckers into your soapy bucket, while laughing maniacally. Mwah-ha-ha!

More Nifty Tips

- Keep your garden tidy. Toss any old stalks, stems, or debris into your compost heap right away to prevent the beasties from making them their home.

- Hose down your crops with water; sometimes a strong spray is all it takes to knock off aphids and other pests once and for all.

- To help catch flying pests, squirt them with soapy water; they'll slow down enough for you to catch them and drop them in your bucket.

Keep Out Critters

• • •

"Squirrels are pretty, but oh my, they can do a lot of damage!"
— BEATRICE NEIDORF

HOW TO REPEL FURRY FRIENDS FROM YOUR GARDEN

Step 1: Identify your uninvited guests. Stake out your garden by sitting very still within eyeshot (camouflage not necessary but totally fun and fashionable) or farther away with a pair of binoculars. Then, check again at night, using the beam of a flashlight to illuminate your patch. If you catch rabbits, squirrels, or deer using your garden as a buffet table, proceed to step 2.

Step 2: Repel the critters. Make your veggies less tasty (for them, not for you) with a hot pepper spray, which is often too fiery for animal (and insect) palates. Buy some or make your own by tossing a few hot chili peppers into your blender with 2 cups water. Blend on high for 2 minutes. Strain the liquid through a cheesecloth into to a spray bottle and top off with water. Shake, and spray on your veggies once a week. (Skip your fruit, as it may leave a slightly peppery flavor.) Another option: Sprinkle mothballs around the perimeter of your garden. See which one works better, or alternate between the two.

Step 3: Distract those furballs. Set up a feeding station, like a bird feeder, far away from your garden to steer their attention away from your crops.

Step 4: Set up a barrier. Try a two-foot-high fence around your garden, or individual mesh cages around each plant. If you've just planted, you can even lay chicken wire directly over the ground.

More Nifty Tips

- Make your yard less appealing to hungry critters by putting lids on your garbage cans and keeping the area clear of debris.

- No hot peppers handy? Try blending a clove of garlic, a small onion, and 1 teaspoon cayenne pepper with water; strain, add water, and spray.

- If you've got burrowing guests, like woodchucks, you may have to bury the bottom of your fences a foot deep. Eventually, they'll give up and go away.

Beat the Grass

. . .

"Every garden needs a fence, because everything eats a garden. Rabbits, squirrels, lambs. Chickens can eat a bed of lettuce in nothing flat. If you get a cow in a garden, the cow can demolish it."
—MILDRED KALISH

HOW TO CHASE A SNAKE OUT OF YOUR GARDEN

Step 1: If you spot a snake in your vegetable patch, get a hold of yourself real quick. If you've got some distance, by all means keep it. If you don't, and the snake is rattling, hissing, or staring you down, freeze until it slithers away. (It will, so long as it has a viable exit. It's more afraid of you than you are of it.) Then exhale, run inside, have a gimlet, share your tale of bravery with all your friends, and then skip to step 4.

Step 2: If you're at a safe distance and you're 100 percent confident in your ability to classify the snakes in your area, then ID your slithering garden guest. If it's poisonous and has made a permanent home in your garden, call an expert to remove it. If it's poisonous and just passing through, wait until it leaves the area and skip to step 4. If it's not at all poisonous, proceed to step 3. If you have absolutely no idea what kind of snake it is, keep your distance, wait for it to leave, and skip to step 4.

Step 3: Decide what you want to do. Some gardeners actually like to keep friendly snakes around, because while they don't eat vegetables or people, they do eat pests, like mice, squirrels, slugs, and earwigs. If that just doesn't cut it for you and you'd rather that nonpoisonous snake find another home, grab a broom and swish it away.

Step 4: Make that snake's return less likely by making your lawn and garden a less fun place for it to live in. Keep your grass short, your hedges trimmed, and your lowest tree branches at least a few feet off the ground. Also, eliminate any mulch or rock piles or fallen logs (after checking them for snakes first!). They make great homes for snakes and their favorite snacks (rodents), and if they're gone, your snake will likely go, too.

More Nifty Tips

- Wear knee-high rubber boots while gardening to protect your ankles (or at least give you a fashionable sense of security).

- Get a cat. Good ones will hunt snakes, or scare them away.

- Know the first-aid procedures for your area. If you live in a place with poisonous snakes, be on guard, and protect yourself and your pets. Keep a snake-bite kit near the backdoor of your house.

Make No Waste

· · ·

*"I can't remember ever throwing things out. We didn't even
have garbage collection where we lived. Scraps were fed to the chickens
or saved for the cats or other critters. Whatever else we had, we
tilled into the garden."*
—ALICE LOFT

HOW TO COMPOST

Step 1: Make a bin. Find a plastic or aluminum garbage can (with
a lid) and drill quarter-inch holes, four to six inches apart, all over
the sides and bottom, so your compost can breathe. If you don't
have a drill, use a hammer and a big nail to pierce each hole. (Don't
make holes in the lid—or in your nose or ears or belly button, unless that's your thing.)

Step 2: Get it started. Almost everything natural can be catego-
rized as either a "brown" or a "green." To make compost happen,
you'll need both colors. Three parts brown to every one part green
works very well. So, start by filling your bin with your "browns," or
carbon-rich material, like fallen leaves (preferably chopped); pine
needles; small twigs; sawdust from untreated, solid wood (not ply-
wood); newspaper, junk mail, or cardboard (all preferably ripped or
shredded).

Step 3: Make it wet. Add enough water until the contents reach
the consistency of a wrung-out sponge.

Step 4: Activate it. Toss in your "greens," or nitrogen-rich material, which includes any fruit or veggie peels, trimmings, or rinds; tea bags; coffee grounds and filters; weeds and lawn clippings. Never add: meat, bones, fish, oil, dairy products, grains, beans, bread, or diseased plants.

Step 5: Protect the process. Top your greens with more browns to keep your bin working properly and smelling fresh. Replace the lid. Keep feeding your bin, always layering one part green with three parts brown, as often as you'd like. Getting down and dirty has never been so much fun!

Step 6: Stir your pile monthly with a pitchfork (or big stick), and wait for about six months until compost forms at the bottom of the barrel. You'll know it's ready when it looks rich, dark, and crumbly (and nothing like what you put into it) and smells earthy.

Step 7: Harvest your compost by tipping the bin. Scoop out the rich dark matter near the bottom, and sprinkle it throughout your garden and around the base of your plants or trees. It's the world's best fertilizer! Plus, it saves money, saves water, and saves the earth from trash. After you're through feeling righteous (and you should), return any not-yet-ready scraps to your bin, replace the lid, and keep it up.

More Nifty Tips

- You can also buy a ready-made compost bin at your local garden store or online.

- For easier stirring, you can tip your bin and roll it on its side so long as the lid fits snugly.

- Save yourself a few trips to the bin by storing your kitchen scraps in a bowl in your fridge or in a ziplock bag in the freezer. When either container gets full, go feed your bin.

- If you're not getting rich compost, your pile may be too dry (add water) or too brown (add "greens" and turn).

- If your pile gets stinky or flies appear, it's either too wet or too green (add "browns" and turn), or you've put something in there that you shouldn't have. Remove any meat, dairy, or grease.

- You can start composting at any time, but autumn may be the best season. Your fall leaves will decompose throughout the winter (composting slows, but doesn't stop, in chilly temps), and you'll be ready for spring planting.

Spice Up Your Life

. . .

"Growing up in Brooklyn, we didn't have a yard, but my father did have a green thumb. He grew a lot of basil in the window. It was amazing what he could do. Fresh herbs, you can't beat them!"
— GRACE FORTUNATO

HOW TO START A WINDOWSILL HERB GARDEN

Step 1: Select your seeds. Chives, cilantro, dill, oregano, basil, lemon verbena, marjoram, plus all the Scarborough Fair types (parsley, sage, rosemary, and thyme) will thrive on a sunny windowsill.

Step 2: Sow your seeds. Grab as many tiny flowerpots (or even two-ounce plastic cups with drainage holes poked in the bottom) as you have seed types, label, and fill with new soil. (A loose mixture of peat moss, vermiculite, and perlite, often sold in garden stores as "potting mix," works well.) Soak your soil thoroughly with warm water. In each pot, sprinkle a few seeds, cover with a quarter inch of soil, give it a gentle pat, and say a few kind words. Then set your pots in a shallow tray partially filled with warm water, and let them sit there for a few minutes until the top layer of soil looks wet.

Step 3: Get your germination on. Turn each pot into a mini greenhouse by covering its top with plastic wrap, secured with a rubber band. Set your pots in a warm spot, like on top of the fridge (it doesn't necessarily have to be bright), and watch for sprouts. It may take up to four weeks. Until then, always keep the soil damp by periodically setting your teensy pots in a shallow water tray. When the top layer of soil looks wet, remove the pot from the tray.

Step 4: Let the sun shine in. Once you see some sprouts, hoot and holler and dance around. Then remove the plastic, move your pots to your sunniest windowsill, and watch your herbs grow, watering (enough so that it runs out the bottom) whenever the top layer of soil feels dry to the touch.

Step 5: After they each sprout about a half-dozen leaves, repot your healthiest herbs in bigger containers, or in a window box—anything with drainage will do. Water and mist your plants whenever the top layer of soil is dry. Just don't overdo it. If your herbs sit in water, they'll rot.

Step 6: Within six to ten weeks, your herbs will be bushy, the leaves will be plentiful, and you can start harvesting! Lick your chops and pinch off the tips for use in your favorite dishes or teas.

More Nifty Tips

- If you've got a few more bucks to spend, well, fancy you! Buy herb seedlings from your garden store and skip steps 1 through 4.

- Mint and oregano tend to be a little pushy, those jerks, so keep them planted in their own containers or they may take over your entire garden.

- Not sure which window is sunniest? Choose the one that faces south. Second best: the one that faces east or west. North-facing windows show the least love.

- Harvest your herbs in the morning for best flavor. Don't feel bad about it, either. Pinching off leaves will only help more grow.

• Is your garden too prolific? First, yay you! Second, harvest your herbs, rinse them in cold water, and chop them up. Then put them in an ice-cube tray, filled with water, and freeze. Transfer herb cubes to ziplock bags and store in the freezer until you're ready for use. (If you're freezing mint cubes, try plunking them directly into your mojito!)

Preserve Knowledge

• • •

"If you had a big garden, you'd preserve everything for the winter. Green beans, corn, peaches, and pears. It was taken pretty seriously. I can see rows and rows of fruit and vegetables in mason jars. It was a nice feeling of accomplishment to see them all lined up."

—Alice Loft

How to Dry Apples

Step 1: Pick some apples. The sweeter, the better. (Think Fujis and Golden Delicious.) You'll also need a few lemons, or lemon juice.

Step 2: Fire up your oven to 140 degrees (or the lowest heat possible), and wash your apples.

Step 3: Mix equal parts lemon juice and water, and then peel, core, and slice your apples into ¼-inch-thick sections. Dunk your apple slices in your lemon water and let them soak for 5 to 10 minutes. It'll help preserve their color.

Step 4: Drain your apples and place each slice about ½ inch apart on a cake rack set on a cookie tray (or, if you don't have a cake rack, just a cookie tray), and pop them in the oven. Set your timer for 5 hours. (Thicker slices may take longer.) Halfway through, ask yourself, How's about them apples? Peek in the oven and check their progress. Flip each slice. And if some are drying faster than others, rotate the trays or shift your oven racks to help evenly distribute the heat. You'll know your apples are done when they're dry and bendy, but not brittle.

Step 5: Let your apples cool, and then throw them in a jar, seal it, and let it sit for a few days, so any remaining moisture will spread out between slices. Shake daily to prevent sticking. (If your jar gets wet, repeat step 4.)

Step 6: Pasteurize your apples by tossing them into ziplock bags and storing them in the freezer for 48 hours. That'll remove any excess moisture and—brace yourself—help kill any fruit fly eggs that may be hanging around.

Step 7: Remove from freezer, and store in a cool, dark place. Your dried apples will be good for 6 months to a year, and eating them will make you feel smart.

More Nifty Tips

- For an added kick, sprinkle cinnamon on your apples before drying.

- No lemons? You can also soak your apples in vitamin C–rich orange or pineapple juice to prevent browning.

- If you dry apples on a cookie tray, be sure to flip them a few times, so air can circulate around both sides.

- If you have a few days and the temps are in the upper 80s or higher, dry your apples in the sun. Set them on a wooden rack or a raised stainless-steel screen (so air can circulate), cover them with cheesecloth (to keep bugs off), and put them on your sunniest windowsill. Take them in at night, and repeat until dry.

Stash Your Bounty

• • •

"If you didn't can your vegetables in the summer, you would do without them in the winter."
—Nikki Spanof Chrisanthon

How to Can Your Own Fruits and Veggies

Step 1: Round up your supplies. You'll need: a water-bath canner (basically a giant pot); two more big pots (one for jars, one for produce); a wire jar-rack (which prevents jar rattling and breakage); a jar-lifter (or some tongs); and enough 1-quart Ball jars, gum-sealed lids, and rings to hold your harvest. (Jars and rings can be reused but lids cannot.)

Step 2: Wash and warm your jars by running them through the dishwasher, or rinsing them with soap and water and heating (not boiling) them in a big water-filled pot (not your canner) on your stove top. (Your jars don't need to be sterilized because once you pack them, you'll boil them for more than 10 minutes.) Prepare your lids according to the manufacturer's instructions. (Some will ask you to heat them, too.)

Prepare your produce, using the instructions on page 53.
...d lids and tightly screw on the rings to secure.

Step 4: Fill your canner with enough water to cover upright jars by at least 1 inch, place a lid on the canner, and bring the water to a boil.

Step 5: Once the water's boiling, remove the lid, set your filled jars in your jar rack, and submerge them in the canner. If the water does not cover jar tops by at least 1 inch, add more *boiling* water. Your jars must *always* be fully submerged, or the contents may spoil. Boo! Replace the canner lid.

Step 6: While maintaining a vigorous boil, set a timer for the appropriate length of boil. (See "Details, Details" on page 53 for produce-by-produce recommendations.)

Step 7: Turn off the heat, remove the canner lid, and wait 5 minutes. Then remove the jars from the canner using a jar-lifter or tongs.

Step 8: Allow the jars to completely cool in an upright position for 12 to 24 hours. Remove the ring on one, hold your breath, and check the lid's seal by pushing on its center. If it pops, the seal is no good. Either replace the lid and boil again within 24 hours, or store in the refrigerator and eat within 2 days.

Step 9: Store in a cool, dry, dark place, away from sunshine and hungry thieves. Most canned fruits and veggies will last at least a year.

Details, Details: Your Produce Guide

Apples: Wash, peel, core, and slice apples. (Nineteen pounds fills seven 1-quart jars.) In a large pot, add 2¼ cups sugar to 9 cups water and bring to boil, stirring constantly until the granules dissolve. Boil the apples in syrup for 5 minutes. Pack the slices and syrup into hot, empty jars, leaving ½ inch space at the top. Seal and boil for 20 minutes.

Peaches: Peel, halve, and pit peaches. (Seventeen and a half pounds fills seven 1-quart jars.) Add 2¼ cups sugar to 9 cups water and bring to a boil, stirring constantly until the granules dissolve. Add the peaches and boil for 5 minutes. Pack the hot peaches in hot, empty jars, and cover with syrup, leaving ½ inch headroom. Seal and boil for 25 minutes.

Tomatoes: Remove skins and halve, or if small, leave whole. (Twenty-one pounds fills seven 1-quart jars.) Pack in jars. Add 2 tablespoons lemon juice to each jar and fill jar to within ½ inch of the top with boiling water or hot tomato juice. Remove any air bubbles with a plastic spatula. Seal and boil for 45 minutes.

Berries: Eat your strawberries fresh (or turn them into jam [see page 55]). They're too low in acid to can without a pressure cooker. For any other kind of berry, wash and remove stems. (Twelve pounds of berries fills seven 1-quart jars.) In a large pot, add 2¼ cups sugar to 9 cups boiling water, stirring constantly until the granules dissolve. Add ½ cup syrup to each hot, empty jar; pack with berries; then top off each jar with more syrup, leaving ½ inch space at the top. (To preserve berries without sugar, replace syrup with boiling water.) Seal and boil for 20 minutes.

More Nifty Tips

- To prevent fruit from browning after cutting, soak in 1 gallon of water mixed with a teaspoon of ascorbic acid or spritz with lemon juice.

- To remove skins from tomatoes and peaches easily, first submerge them in boiling water for 45 seconds and then plunge them into ice water. The skin'll slide right off!

- All the fruit here is packed in light syrup. To make the syrup less sweet, add 1¼ cups sugar to 10½ cups water. To make it even sweeter, add 3¾ cups sugar to 8¼ cups water.

- All boiling times are good at sea level. If you're above 1,000 feet, add 5 minutes to your boil. Above 3,000 feet, add 10. Above 6,000 feet, add 15.

- For recipes, how-tos, and basically everything you could ever want to know about canning, visit the National Center for Home Food Preservation at www.uga.edu/nchfp/.

Sweeten Your Day

• • •

"I'd go to the briar patch, pick blackberries, and make jam. We'd eat it on pancakes, buns, and biscuits. You don't even have to can it, because you'll eat it so fast."
—Mildred Kalish

How to Make (and Can) Strawberry Jam

Step 1: Pick your own berries. You'll need about 4½ pints' worth (or 9 cups) for every batch of jam you make. It's okay if a few of them are underripe. They'll help your jam set.

Step 2: Gather your supplies and other ingredients. You'll need: 2 large lemons, 4 cups sugar, a large pot, a wooden spoon, a small plate, and, if you don't plan on finishing off your jam immediately, all the usual canning supplies, including a canner (aka a ginormous pot), a wire jar-rack (to help prevent breakage), a jar-grabber (or tongs), a ladle, and four ½-pint canning jars with new lids and rings.

Step 3: Put your little plate in the freezer. You'll need it later for something very interesting. Cue the up-and-down eyebrows.

Step 4: To sterilize your jars, fill your canner with hot water. Place your empty jars in your jar rack, submerge them in the water, and boil for 10 minutes. Prepare your lids and rings according to the manufacturer's instructions. Turn off the heat but leave your jars submerged in the hot water for now.

Step 5: Wash your strawberries, and remove their caps.

Step 6: Toss your berries into a large pot and gently (or depending on your mood, not so gently) crush them with your wooden spoon, leaving some berries smushed but fairly recognizable. Simmer over low to medium heat for 10 minutes.

Step 7: Add the sugar, plus ⅓ cup freshly squeezed lemon juice, stirring constantly until the sugar dissolves.

Step 8: Crank up the heat to bring your berry mixture to a boil. Keep it bubbling for about 20 minutes, or until it starts to thicken. Don't worry. This part is not as boring as it sounds, because you've got two big jobs: Stir frequently to save those unlucky berries on the bottom from burning, and scoop off any foam that collects on top.

Step 9: Retrieve your plate from the freezer, and test the thickness of your jam by dropping a teaspoon of jam onto it. Count to 30, hold your breath, and then tip the plate. If the mixture gels and moves only slightly, proceed to step 10. If it runs down the plate, refreeze your plate, say a few choice curse words, boil your jam for another 1 to 2 minutes, and test again. Repeat as necessary.

Step 10: Remove the jam from heat. Using tongs, remove your sterilized jars from the hot water and shake to empty them. Using a ladle, fill your jars, leaving ¼ inch of headroom. Wipe off any drips from the rim, using a clean, damp paper towel, to get a good seal. Add the lid, and screw on the ring to secure. Repeat until all the jars are full.

Step 11: Now you need to preserve your jam. Double-check the water level in your canner; it must be deep enough to fully cover the upright jars by at least 2 inches. Bring the water to a boil. Using your tongs, lower your jars into your jar rack and submerge them in the boiling water, cover the canner with the lid, and boil for 5 minutes. Turn off the heat, and wait 5 more minutes.

Step 12: Transfer your jars with tongs to your rack and let cool for 12 to 24 hours. Check the seal by pressing the center of each lid. If it doesn't pop, it's good! Store in a cool, dark place for up to a year. If it does pop, repeat step 11 within 24 hours or put that jar in the fridge and use right away.

More Nifty Tips

- For faster berry crushing, swap your wooden spoon for a potato masher.

- If you don't trust the chilled-plate test, double-check yourself using a kitchen thermometer. When your jam reaches 220 degrees, it's ready to jar.

- Have a not-quite-full jar after step 10? Put a lid on it and stick it in the fridge. It'll be good for 3 to 4 weeks.

- Some people use pectin to set their jam. That works, too! Just follow the instructions on the box.

- Add lemon or orange zest during step 7 for added pop.

Buy Locally
. . .

"My mother would go to the farmers' market on Saturday, and go from stand to stand to see where she could get the best price."
—Nikki Spanof Chrisanthon

HOW TO SHOP AT THE FARM

Step 1: Join a CSA. Community Supported Agriculture allows neighbors to buy shares, in advance, in a local farmer's harvest in exchange for a weekly delivery of produce from the farm, usually from June through November. To find a participating farm near you, visit FoodRoutes.org.

Step 2: Frequent your local farmers' market or roadside stand. There's nothing fresher or better tasting than fruit and veggies that have traveled only as far as from the field to the edge of the road. No trucks, no refrigerators, no warehouses. That's better for you, the farmer, and the environment. To find a nearby market, visit FoodRoutes.org or LocalHarvest.org.

Step 3: Go straight to the farm. Visit a pick-your-own, and harvest your own crops with your own hands. It's fun, it's cheaper, and you'll appreciate every bite much more than you can imagine. To find a farmer who won't call the cops when you show up with your own basket, visit PickYourOwn.org.

More Nifty Tips

- Chat up your local farmer. Oftentimes, he'll sell windfall apples for super cheap.

- Hit the farmers' market late in the day. They usually drop the prices before closing so they don't have to haul their produce home.

Cleaning

. . .

Take responsibility for your own mess.
Use environmentally friendly products, and
never pay someone to do what you can do for yourself.

Cure Wrinkles

· · ·

"My dad had a candy store, and he used to get hundred-pound bags of sugar. When the sugar was gone, my mom would bleach the bags in the sun and make sheets out of them."
—Nikki Spanof Chrisanthon

How to Properly Fold a Fitted Sheet

Step 1: With the sheet entirely inside out, place your left hand into any corner and your right hand into the next closest corner.

Step 2: Bringing your hands together, flip the corner on your right hand over the corner on your left. (Your right hand will be free and your left hand will be holding two corners.)

Step 3: Transfer both corners to your right hand, run your left hand down the length of the sheet, and nest the two remaining corners together with your left hand.

Step 4: With two corners on each hand, bring your hands together and flip the corners from your right hand onto your left hand.

Step 5: Grasp the right edge. Gently shake out the sheet, allowing the elasticized edges to fall toward you. Lay on a flat surface (the sheet, not you).

Step 6: Fold in thirds, lengthwise, and then in half.

Step 7: Smooth, place the sheet on the shelf, and beam with pride.

More Nifty Tips

• This one takes some practice. If you get stuck, lay your sheet down during step 3. You'll master it in no time!

Catch Some Z's

・・・

*"You were expected to make your bed every day. My mom always said,
'Throw your covers back. Get the sleep out of it. Let it cool and
then make your bed.' "*
—ALICE LOFT

HOW TO MAKE A BED

Step 1: Place a mattress pad on top of the mattress for added protection and comfort. You can even get waterproof ones, if any sleepyheads in your bed are prone to, you know, accidents.

Step 2: Lay your fitted sheet on the mattress, tucking the top two corners fully *beneath* the top two corners of the mattress. Repeat at the bottom of the bed. If you don't do the full tuck-under, your sheet may come loose during the night. Total nightmare! Smooth it out with your hands.

Step 3: Standing alongside the bed and holding the long side of your flat sheet (hemmed edge at the top) with two hands, snap it in the air and let it spread over the mattress. Make sure the sheet is centered and each edge runs parallel to the floor. Walk to the foot of the bed and pull the sheet down, so the top of the sheet meets the top of the bed and the bottom drapes about a foot over the end.

Step 4: To make tight corners, tuck the bottom of the sheet under the mattress. Then grasp the side of the sheet about 15 inches from the bottom, lift it out to the side, and then lay it on top of the mattress. Tuck the loose, hanging edge underneath the mattress, and then flip your corner down, pulling it taut and tucking it under.

Step 5: Lay a quilt, blanket, or down comforter over the top.

Step 6: Slide your pillows into cases and lay them at the head of the bed.

More Nifty Tips

- Flip your mattress each season, and rotate it twice a year, to help prevent sagging.

- If you have a feather bed, shake it out before making the bed, to add fluff.

- Use sheets that are the same size as your mattress: twin sheets for a twin bed, queen sheets for a queen bed, and so on. If they're too big or too small, you won't be comfy. Duh!

- To freshen up your sheets, spritz them with lavender linen spray; you'll drift off to la-la land more quickly. To freshen up your pillows, set them in the sun.

Save Your Silkies

· · ·

"We hud a washtub, a big old yellow bar of soap, and a rub board. So we'd rub our clothes on that board and hang them on the line to dry. We felt proud of our clean clothes, or I wouldn't have done it."
—Elouise Bruce

HOW TO HAND WASH DELICATES

Step 1: Gather your delicates: silks, lacy numbers, stockings, knits that may shrink, or any items with fancy accoutrement that could get damaged in a spin cycle. Unless the tag says DRY CLEAN ONLY, you can hand wash them yourself at home. Sort by color.

Step 2: Fill a basin with room-temperature water (too hot and your color may bleed; too cold and your clothes may not come clean). Add just a squirt of mild liquid detergent, like Woolite, and swish.

Step 3: Submerge your lightest-colored items in the tub and let soak for about 3 minutes. Swirl and dip if you must, but never rub, twist, or wring.

Step 4: Remove your clothing from the basin and give it a gentle squeeze. (Again, never—snicker, snicker—twist your delicates.) Set it on a clean, light-colored towel. If you have more to wash, proceed from lightest to darkest.

Step 5: Empty and rinse your wash basin, and refill with it clean water. Swirl each item of clothing to rinse, proceeding again from lightest to darkest. Repeat, if necessary.

Step 6: Lay each item on a clean, light-colored towel again, restoring each delicate to its original shape. Roll up the towel, from bottom to top, pressing gently to remove any excess water from your delicates.

Step 7: Hang item to dry, if possible, or lay flat on a towel and turn it over halfway through the process.

More Nifty Tips

• Turn a fan on your delicates to speed the drying time.

• No gentle detergent? Try a spot of baby shampoo.

Harness the Wind

· · ·

"I don't know why there is such a big satisfaction in drying your clothes in the sun and air. When you gather them in, you're gathering in freshness."
—Mildred Kalish

How to Install a Clothesline

Step 1: Find a private spot. No one, especially your neighbor, wants to stare at your undies blowing in the breeze for three seasons out of the year. A location with a mix of sun and shade might work best, because strong rays can bleach whites (yay!) but fade colors (boo!).

Step 2: Decide how fancy you want to get.

Not at all fancy: A cotton rope tied between two trees, about three to four inches above your head height, will get the job done.

Sort of fancy: Tie a rope around a tree, just above head height; screw a heavy-duty metal hook into your porch (or garage or barn) at the same level; and attach a cleat on the wall about 6 inches below. (If you don't know what a cleat is, stick to the not-at-all-fancy version. It dries your clothes just as well.) To run the line, thread the rope from the tree through the hook and wrap it around the cleat several times to tighten and secure it. When not in use, simply coil your rope near the base of the tree or hang it on a branch.

Very fancy: Buy two clothesline poles at your local hardware store, some rope, and a bag of cement. Dig two holes in the ground about 1 foot wide and at least 1 foot deep in your desired location. Prepare your cement according to the instructions on the bag. Spray one hole with water, fill it halfway with cement, plumb your pole, and then top off with cement. Repeat on the other end. Allow your cement to dry for at least 24 hours, and then run your line.

Step 3: That's it! As you hang your wet laundry out to dry, feel good knowing that you're saving money—and the environment.

More Nifty Tips

- Run your line north to south for the most rays.

- Don't hang it under a bird's nest, or your clean clothes may become dirty very quickly.

- Snap your clothes after taking them down to soften them (and to look cool).

- If your clothesline starts to sag and your wet laundry starts to drag, build a prop: Hammer two nails into the top of an old broom handle and wedge the handle between the line and the ground for a boost.

Get Hot and Fresh

· · ·

"Your life depended on how good a housekeeper you were. If you were competent, life was pleasant."
—Ruth Rowen

How to Clean an Oven

·

Step 1: Remove your oven racks and let them soak for several hours in hot, soapy water. Scour, rinse, and dry.

Step 2: Check your oven's capabilities. If you see a button or dial that says CLEAN, you're in luck! You have a self-cleaning oven, which means all you have to do is set it to CLEAN, let it cool, and then use a damp sponge to wipe out any ash that may collect on the bottom. If yours doesn't have a self-cleaning feature, no pouting. You'll have it fresh and sparkly in no time.

Step 3: Scrape out any major spills with a plastic spatula. This part is more fun if you can remember how great whatever it is you're scraping tasted back when you ate it.

Step 4: Add 3 tablespoons baking soda to a spray bottle and fill with warm water. Shake to mix, and spritz on all of your oven's inner surfaces. Let sit for 10 minutes.

Step 5: Wipe out with a damp sponge. Repeat as necessary.

More Nifty Tips

- Wipe out spills as soon as they happen to make cleaning easier in the future.

- Can't get to them? Sprinkle salt over the mess and wipe clean after the oven cools.

- For an especially greasy oven window, wipe it down with a damp and soapy sponge. Then scrape clean with a razor blade. Intense, yes, but very effective!

Get Your Sparkle On

. . .

*"We always did the dishes. There were three girls in my family
and we traded off every week. One washed, one wiped, one put away.
That was a given."*
—ALICE LOFT

HOW TO PROPERLY HAND WASH DISHES

Step 1: Scrape excess food off your dishes, rinse with hot water,
and stack them next to the sink. Place a drying rack on the other side
of the sink. Turn on some music or recruit a chatty friend for company.

Step 2: Fill your basin with soap and the hottest water you can
physically stand.

Step 3: Squirt a drop of soap onto a rag, and scrub-a-dub-dub dishes according to their grease content: cups and glasses first, silverware second, plates and bowls next, pots and pans last.

Step 4: Rinse with hot water, set in the rack to dry, and admire your reflection.

More Nifty Tips

- Wearing rubber gloves will help keep your skin soft and allow you to wash in hotter water, ensuring cleaner dishes.

- When washing china, place a dish towel at the bottom of the sink. If you happen to drop a piece, it'll be less likely to break.

Shine On

• • •

"Every Saturday, my mother cleaned the downstairs and my sister and I had to clean the second floor. In those days, we had aluminum floors, so our job was to scrub the floors and the stairs leading downstairs."
—NIKKI SPANOF CHRISANTHON

HOW TO MOP

Step 1: Send everyone with pitter-pattering feet packing, move any furniture that's in your way, and put on some good music. Remember, the word *mop* doesn't end with an *e*.

Step 2: Sweep the floor to remove any dust or dirt, which can scratch your floors and literally muck up the works.

Step 3: Fill a bucket with cold water and add a squirt of dishwashing detergent.

Step 4: Dunk your mop, thoroughly wring it out, and go to it, starting in the far corner of your room. On polyurethaned hardwood floors, run your mop with the grain of the wood. (Never mop waxed hardwood floors; the water may cause damage.) For textured floors, move your mop in small figure eights.

Step 5: Once you finish a section or when your mop starts looking dirty, wring it out over your bucket, dunk it, wring once more, and continue mopping.

Step 6: Once you've finished the job, dump your mop water into the toilet (so you don't dirty your sink) and flush. Peek at your sparkling floors, but don't step on them, not even on tiptoe, until they're dry.

More Nifty Tips

- Use a cotton mop for textured floors, like brick or slate, and a sponge mop for smooth surfaces, like hardwood or linoleum.

- Plan your exit strategy before starting, so you don't mop yourself into a corner.

- To mop hallways, go along the baseboard first and then do the middle.

Get a Clean Slate

. . .

*"I doubt that we ever bought anything specifically for any chores. There
was always soap and water and vinegar in the house."*
—ALICE LOFT

HOW TO KILL MILDEW

On Clothes

Step 1: Take your dank clothes outside and brush off any black
fuzz you might see.

Step 2: Make a paste of lemon juice and salt and spread on the
spotted area.

Step 3: Leave your clothes in the sun for several hours. If you
have a clothesline (see page 69), hang them up. Otherwise, lay them
flat on a clean, dry surface.

Step 4: Rinse thoroughly with water, and then launder as usual.

On Books

Step 1: It's perfectly acceptable to cry over your mildewed books.
Just don't let your tears fall on the pages. Moisture and warmth pro-
mote mold.

Step 2: After you regain your composure, take your books outside on a sunny day. With a dry towel, gently brush the damaged pages.

Step 3: Very lightly dust the pages with cornstarch, set the books on end, and leave in the fresh air for several hours.

Step 4: Brush your pages once more, and start reading.

On Furniture

Step 1: Check for change between the cushions, and do with it what you will. (For suggestions, see page 222.)

Step 2: Give your couch or chair a good once-over with your vacuum.

Step 3: Carry the item outside on a sunny, not-too-humid day and let the sun do its work. A few black spores are no match for powerful UV rays. Sha-zam!

On Painted Walls

Step 1: Put on some rubber gloves. (Do it with a dramatic snapping motion to increase your pleasure.)

Step 2: Pour ¾ cup bleach into a gallon of water, and with a clean sponge, wipe down your walls.

Step 3: Rinse out your sponge with fresh water, and wipe the walls once more.

On Bathroom Tiles

Step 1: Spray or wipe your tiles with a solution of four parts water to one part vinegar, and go do something else, preferably something much more fun, for an hour or so. (You can also use straight vinegar, but do it too frequently and it may break down your grout.)

Step 2: Sprinkle baking soda on a stiff brush (or a toothbrush) and go nuts on your walls, scrubbing all the grout lines vigorously.

Step 3: Rinse and, if necessary, repeat.

More Nifty Tips

• Keep your home clean and well ventilated. Mildew thrives in dirty, dark, and moist places. Open your windows on breezy days. Don't put dirty or wet clothes in your closet. Turn on your bathroom fan. And think about new ways to let the sun shine in!

Take the Cheese

• • •

"We had rats, and I was grossed out. My father would take some Italian bread, toast it, put olive oil on it, and set that on the trap as a bait. It worked! But to this day, if I see a mouse, I run."
— GRACE FORTUNATO

HOW TO RID YOUR HOUSE OF MICE

Step 1: Clean up. Sure, you're an exceedingly interesting person, but the only reason mice (those moochers!) will want to visit you is for the free food. If you don't offer them any, they'll be less likely to shack up with you. So, leave no crumb behind. Wipe off your countertop and sweep your kitchen floor when you're through cooking. Don't eat potato chips on the couch (or crackers in bed). Cover or take out your trash. Store edibles, like cereal and even dog food, in air-tight containers. And if you see any mouse poop, clean that up, too.

Step 2: Find their entry points. Check for holes (¼ inch or larger) along your walls, underneath your cabinets, between your floorboards and baseboards, and especially around lighting and plumbing fixtures. Don't forget to peek behind the stove and refrigerator! Stuff any crevices you find with steel wool. Mice can't chew through it.

Step 3: Pour a few drops of peppermint oil (available at most health food stores or grocers) onto cotton balls and place them around the house, particularly in places where you think mice may frequent, like behind your stove, under your sinks, along your walls, near your trash can, or around your heating vents. The minty-fresh smell will make you feel peppy and make your mice feel overwhelmed. Their schnozes are just too sensitive.

Step 4: If all else fails, set traps along your walls, which is where mice prefer to run. Snap traps are the most humane because they kill instantly. Glue traps are mean because they don't. And no-kill traps will keep your mice alive, at least until you relocate them to a field, where, sad to say, their chances may be slim anyway.

More Nifty Tips

- Plant peppermint around your doors and in window boxes (see page 46 for instructions) to help make your house less welcoming to Mickey, Minnie, and their no-good cousins.
- Get a kitty.

Freshen Up

. . .

"Spring cleaning was a big event. The first thing you'd do after you'd done it was to tell everybody that you'd finished. They'd all be so envious."
—Mildred Kalish

How to Spring Clean

Step 1: Schedule it. Spring cleaning isn't something you should start on a whim. You've got to get into the proper mind-set. Block off a weekend (or more, if you're in it alone), stock up on cleaning supplies (including paper towels, baking soda, and vinegar), make an excellent playlist, and think about how refreshed you'll feel when everything is spiffed up and in order.

Step 2: Make a checklist, room by room, of tasks to be completed. In each room, you'll need to: dust every surface (including your walls, ceiling, and ceiling fans); wipe down dirty walls (using a sponge, water, and a squirt of dishwashing detergent); mop or vacuum (even under and behind furniture): steam clean your rugs if necessary; wash your light fixtures; take down and wash your drapes or blinds; beat your cushions, rugs, pillows, and mats (outside); and clean your windows inside *and* out (including your screens). It sounds sucky and a bit overwhelming, but just tackle it bit by bit. Yes, it's hard, but most good things in life are.

Step 3: Add room-by-room specialty tasks to your list. In the kitchen, wipe out the fridge, defrost and wipe out your freezer, clean your oven, and organize your pantry and drawers. In the bedroom, flip and rotate your mattress, switch your bedding, wash your pillows, and swap your winter clothes for summer clothes, donating anything you no longer wear. In the bathroom, add your weekly tasks, like scrubbing your toilet, shower, and sinks, plus clean out your medicine cabinet, tossing any expired goods. In the office, remove your books from shelves and dust, wipe down computers, and organize your important papers.

Step 4: Prioritize your tasks to decide which ones you'd like to tackle first. If you have help, start delegating. If not, dive in, making sure you can finish what you start, lest you create a bigger mess.

More Nifty Tips

- Change the batteries in your smoke and carbon monoxide detectors, too. You should do it twice a year.

- To dust high-up spaces, wrap an old T-shirt around the end of a broom.

Clean Naturally

. . .

"Vinegar is like a miracle cleaner."
—BEATRICE NEIDORF

HOW TO USE VINEGAR
TO CLEAN ALMOST ANYTHING

To Disinfect

Step 1: If you're feeling a little Howard Hughes–ish, just fill a spray bottle with white distilled vinegar and spritz anything germy: doorknobs, phones, cupboard handles, sinks, and toilet seats.

Step 2: Wipe clean with a damp cloth.

Step 3: Lick to test. Just kidding! Don't do that!

To Shine Windows

Step 1: Mix one part vinegar with one part water in a spray bottle.

Step 2: Squirt on windows.

Step 3: Wipe clean.

Step 4: Check out your reflection. Wink at yourself. Hope no one else saw you.

To Clean a Kitchen Sink

Step 1: Roll up your sleeves and, if what you see is grossing you out, put on some gloves.

Step 2: Combine a squirt of liquid soap, ¼ cup baking soda, and a splash of vinegar to form a creamy paste.

Step 3: Apply it to your sink basin. Scrub and rinse.

To Freshen the Air in the Bathroom

Step 1: Open a window, and vow to never eat *that* again.

Step 2: Add 1 tablespoon vinegar, 1 teaspoon baking soda, and 1 cup of water to a spray bottle.

Step 3: Mist away!

To Clean the Toilet

Step 1: Pour 1 cup vinegar into the bowl, and let stand for at least 5 minutes.

Step 2: Scrub the toilet with a stiff brush.

Step 3: Flush-a-roo.

To Remove Glass Rings from Wood

Step 1: Mix 2 tablespoons vinegar with 2 tablespoons vegetable oil.

Step 2: Dab a soft rag into the solution and then rub the wood, along the grain, to make the ring disappear.

Step 3: Get out your coasters!

To Undo Accidents

Step 1: Look around to see who has wet pants and get the poor culprit into dry clothes pronto.

Step 2: Mix equal parts vinegar and water, spray on the wee spot, and scrub with a towel.

Step 3: Sprinkle the tinkle with baking soda, and let dry.

Step 4: Brush or vacuum the spot.

To Clean Toys

Step 1: Fill a basin with soapy water and add a splash of vinegar.

Step 2: Wrest the toys away from your baby, preferably when she's not looking.

Step 3: Soak, rinse, dry, and give them back, you ogre.

To Whiten Your Whites

Step 1: Add ¼ cup vinegar to your whites during the final rinse to help remove any soapy residue from your duds. It'll also soften fabrics and reduce static cling.

Step 2: Go relax. There's nothing else for you to see here.

To Remove Sweat Stains

Step 1: Spray vinegar directly on the collar and pits of your shirts.

Step 2: Wash as you usually would.

To De-smoke Clothes

Step 1: Your clothes better not smell like an ashtray because you had a cigarette hanging out of your mouth all night. If that's the case, vow to quit that nasty habit right now. If that's not the case, who are you hanging out with? Hooligans, that's who.

Step 2: Hang your smoky clothes on your shower rod.

Step 3: Fill your bathtub with steaming hot water, and add 1 cup vinegar.

Step 4: Shut your bathroom door, and let the steam infiltrate (and freshen) your clothes.

Clean More Stuff Naturally

. . .

"There was no man's work or woman's work. There was only work, and anybody who was around was expected to chip in."
—LUCILE FRISBEE

HOW TO USE BAKING SODA AROUND THE HOUSE

To Absorb Odors

Step 1: Identify stinky places—say, your fridge, your trash cans, your gym bag, your hamper.

Step 2: Set a breathable box of baking soda inside (it won't spill), or if your smelly stuff is about to be washed anyway (ahem, your dirty laundry), sprinkle it directly on top.

To Polish Silver

Step 1: Inherit some silver or go buy some at a garage sale.

Step 2: Make a paste of three parts baking soda and one part water.

Step 3: Rub into silver with a soft cloth.

Step 4: Rinse with water and dry.

To Clean Your Countertops

Step 1: Wipe away any crumbs or spills.

Step 2: Sprinkle some baking soda on a damp cloth and scrub.

Step 3: Rinse with a clean damp cloth or sponge.

To Refresh Your Rugs

Step 1: Sprinkle baking soda directly onto your shag and let sit for 15 minutes.

Step 2: Suck it up (with a vacuum).

Step 3: Take a whiff and be pleased.

To De-crust Pots and Pans

Step 1: Sprinkle some baking soda on the gunk.

Step 2: Fill pan with hot water, and let soak overnight.

Step 3: Scrape off the crust in the morning and be amazed at how easily it comes off.

Step 4: Vow to set a timer the next time you cook so you won't burn food onto the bottoms of your pans anymore.

To Freshen Fido or Fifi

Step 1: If you can't swing a full-on bubble bath, sprinkle some baking soda directly on your dog or cat's fur and brush it through.

Step 2: Sprinkle some more on her bed and, if she has one, in her litter box, too.

Step 3: Put a bow or bandana around her neck. It won't do anything for the smell, but she'll look so cute and that'll make it a little better.

To Clean Up Grease Spills

Step 1: Sprinkle baking soda directly on the spill, whether it's in your kitchen or your garage.

Step 2: Scrub with a wet brush or rag.

To Extinguish a Fire

Step 1: Try to remain calm and collected. It's time for action. You can freak out later.

Step 2: To put out the flames, scatter baking soda all over them. It works on any kind of fire, including electrical and grease fires.

Step 3: Check yourself and your surroundings for damage.

Step 4: Freak out now, if you must, but then give yourself a pat on the back for averting disaster.

To Clean the Grill

Step 1: Get a little girl-on-grill action going by sprinkling baking soda directly on your rack.

Step 2: Then remove the rack and soak it for a couple of hours to overnight in hot, soapy water.

Step 3: Scrub with a wire brush and return to the grill.

To Spruce Up Your Patio Furniture

Step 1: Mix ¼ cup baking soda with 1 quart warm water.

Step 2: Using a soft rag, wipe down your chaise with the solution.

Step 3: Go over it once more using a clean, damp rag.

Step 4: Relax and rejoice. Summertime is here!

Dressing

· · ·

*You can look fantastic without running up
your credit cards. Be smart about what you buy.
Take care of what you own, and wear it
until you wear it out.*

Save Your Shirt

. . .

"My grandma taught me how to sew a big button on a navy peacoat when I was ten years old. I was very proud of myself. From then on I was sewing buttons on everyone's shirts."
—MILDRED KALISH

HOW TO SEW A BUTTON

Step 1: Gather your supplies. You'll need a replacement button, a needle, about two feet of matching thread, and a pair of scissors.

Step 2: Thread the needle, pulling one end of the thread through to meet the other. Knot the ends together by making a loop and pulling the tails through. Knot once more, and trim off any excess.

Step 3: Locate your button's proper spot by eyeballing where it was before it fell off. Look for either some old broken thread (and remove it) or a few tiny holes in the fabric from where the thread once was. If you can see where it should go, fasten your other buttons, pass a pin through the hole of the renegade, and mark that spot with chalk or pencil.

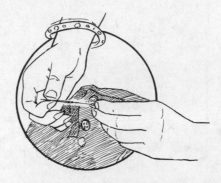

Step 4: Push your needle up through the back of the fabric to the front, pulling the thread all the way through. Slide your button on down the thread to meet the fabric.

Step 5: Once you've got your button in place and the holes lined up, push your needle down through the opposite hole (either diagonally or adjacently to match your other buttons) and out the back of the fabric. Repeat four times, pulling the thread tight enough so that your button doesn't dangle but loose enough so that your fabric doesn't pucker. If you have a four-hole button, switch hole-pairs and repeat.

Step 6: For the finishing touch, push your needle up through the back of the fabric to the front but *not* through any buttonholes. Just let it dangle out the side. Pull your button away from the fabric and wrap your thread tightly around the shank (aka the thread between the button and fabric) six times.

Step 7: Press your needle through the shank twice. Snip the thread—no need to knot.

Step 8: Get dressed, feel proud, look snazzy.

More Nifty Tips

- Check inside your shirt for replacement buttons. Manufacturers, at least the nice ones, will stash a few extras inside, usually along the side or bottom seam.

- If you lose a noticeable button, can't find a replacement, and are just hanging in the wind, snip one from a less-conspicuous spot, like the very bottom of your shirt or a cuff, preferably one you'll later roll up. That'll buy you a little time to replace the button.

- If you're sewing a button onto a thicker fabric, place a matchstick or toothpick on the button and sew over it to help you maintain proper spacing. Then remove the spacer before winding the thread around the shank.

Measure Up

• • •

"My mother made our clothes. She'd buy the material, but some people used flour sacks. No one was better than anyone else. That's what you had and that was it."
—JEAN DINSMORE

HOW TO HEM YOUR FANCY PANTS

Step 1: Round up your stuff: a needle, some thread that matches your pants, a handful of straight pins, an iron, a ruler, chalk or a pencil, and scissors. Fire up your iron. And find a full-length mirror.

Step 2: Slip on your too-long trousers, plus whatever fabulous shoes you intend to wear with them. On the outside of your right foot, fold your hem underneath so your pants hang a proper ¼ inch off the floor. Secure with two straight pins, placed horizontally, one at the top of the fold and one at the bottom. (Your pants will rise when you bend over so after you pin, stand up straight, arms by your sides, to double-check the length.)

Step 3: Take off your pants. Woo hoo! Sewing in your undies is fun! Peek inside your pinned pant leg and, using a ruler, measure the length of the material you've folded up inside. Using that measurement as your guide, fold up and pin around the entire leg. Repeat on the other pant leg.

Step 4: Iron your new hems on the inside of your pant leg, pressing to form a new crease. Try on your trousers again to triple-check the length. If they're too long or short, no sweat! Just go back to step 2 and give it another whirl.

Step 5: Take off your pants, remove the pins, turn your pants inside out, and unfold your new hem. Don't worry—the crease will remain. Then rip out the old hem by very carefully snipping every few stitches and removing the loose threads between snips.

Step 6: Lay your pants flat, in-seam to in-seam, and from the crease that marks your new hem, measure down 1¼ inches (for straight-legged pants) or ¾ inch (for tapered or flared pants). Mark it with chalk or a pencil in several places, connect dots with a straightedge, and then cut along that line to trim the excess. Fold your new bottom edge inward by ¼ inch and iron in that teensy crease so it's nice and neat. (This whole razzle-madazzle will help prevent any frayed edges.)

Step 7: Now that you're free from any excess pantage, fold up your new hem again, using your handy crease as your guide, and repin it every few inches, placing pins perpendicular to the new hem.

Step 8: Measure out about three feet of thread, roughly the distance between your nose and fingertips. (If you've got unusually short arms, turn your head to the left while measuring out to the right for added distance. If you've also got an unusually large nose, you may end up with extra thread, but that's okay.) Thread your needle by passing the end you snipped from the spool through the eye and pulling it down, until it's about twice as long as the straggling end. (Doing it this way will help avoid tangles.) You're going to sew with a single strand of thread, so rather than knotting both strands of thread together, just make a little knot at the end of the single, long strand, while allowing the short strand to continue dangling.

Step 9: Hooray! It's actually time to sew. Place your needle underneath the very edge of your new hem and press it up through the fabric. (Your thread's knot will be hidden beneath your hem.) Move along the hem about a pinky's width, and make your first real stitch by passing your needle through just a few threads of the cloth of your pant leg (just above the fold) and then up through the fold of your hem. Move down ½ inch, and repeat. Make sure you're putting your needle through only the tiniest bit of fabric on the leg of your pants; this will make the stitches nearly invisible.

Step 10: After every third completed stitch, lock your work by passing your needle and thread once more through the fold only before continuing on. (This little trick will help prevent the entire hem from unraveling, if you ever get your heel caught in it.)

Step 11: Once you stitch all the way around your pant leg, press your needle up through the fold only, as you've done on every third stitch, and pass it underneath the resulting loop before you pull it taut to form a knot. Repeat twice, and trim any excess thread.

Step 12: Turn your pants right side out, iron the hem once more for added crispness, and strut your stuff.

More Nifty Tips

- Don't pull your thread too tight, or your pants will pucker up, and not in a good way.

- If you can't find matching thread, always use a shade darker, not lighter. It'll be less noticeable.

Smooth Things Over

* * *

"When I tell you we ironed, we ironed every last thing that came out of the wash, including our sheets and underwear!"
—GRACE FORTUNATO

HOW TO IRON A SHIRT

Step 1: Set up your ironing board in a clean, uncluttered spot next to an outlet. Fill your iron with water and plug it in. Crank it to the appropriate temperature, as recommended on the label of your shirt. If your iron is too hot, you'll torch your top. Too cold, and you'll lose the war on wrinkles.

Step 2: Pop the collar as if it were 1983. Lay your unbuttoned shirt, faceup, on the board and spread the collar flat. Using small circular motions, iron the collar from the center toward each point. Flip it and repeat.

Step 3: Do the yoke. Pull the shoulder of your shirt over the pointy end of the board, and iron the piece of material that connects the collar to the body. Switch shoulders and repeat.

Step 4: Smooth the sleeves. Grab the right one and, aligning the seam along the underarm, from pit to cuff, spread it flat on the board. Work your iron in tiny circles from shoulder to (but not over) cuff.

Step 5: Cock the cuffs. Spread them flat and iron from the sleeve's seam to the edge. Flip it, and repeat. If you have folded cuffs, fold now and iron just the crease.

Step 6: Iron the front and back. If you're right-handed, drape the right panel of your shirt's front over the board, collar toward the pointy end, allowing the rest of the shirt to hang in front of you. (If you're a lefty, start with the left front panel.) Work your iron in small circular motions from the top to the tail. Rotate the shirt over the board to iron the back. Rotate again to iron the front left panel.

Step 7: Wear immediately or hang on a hanger, preferably a wooden one.

More Nifty Tips

- Iron only clean shirts. If you try to press a dirty one, you could set in stains—mwah-ha-ha!—forever.

- Spritz stubborn wrinkles with a water bottle before ironing.

- To iron around buttons, poke the point of your iron, held flat, between each, angling up and down with every pass. Don't plow over them or they could break.

Toast Your Tootsies

...

"I tried to darn the holes in my husband's socks. They'd always come out lumpy, but his feet were warm."
—SUE WESTHEIMER RANSOHOFF

HOW TO DARN WOOL SOCKS

Step 1: Grab a darning needle (aka tapestry needle) (aka a thick, blunt needle) and find some yarn that matches your holey sock—or some yarn that doesn't, if you're a little kooky.

Step 2: Measure off about three to four feet of yarn, from your nose to your fingertips and then some, and thread your needle, pulling your yarn through so that one end is long and the other is just a few inches.

Step 3: Turn your sock inside out and slip a wooden darning mushroom (or, if you don't have one, a tennis or golf ball) inside. Gently spread the sock's hole over the curved top of your darning tool or ball, so you can get a good look at the damage done.

Step 4: Stitch a circle around the hole, about an inch larger in diameter than the hole, by weaving your needle over and under every stitch.

Step 5: Patch the hole with a plain basket weave. Starting on, say, the left, weave your needle over and under every knitted stitch from the bottom of the stitched circle to the top. When you get to the top, leave a teeny loop (so your socks have give), move one row to the right, and weave your way back to the bottom of your stitched circle. Repeat. Depending on the thickness of your socks, you'll probably fit in a few rows before you get to the hole itself. When you're weaving the rows broken by the hole, simply jump your needle to the other side and continue weaving. This will result in parallel lines of yarn over the hole.

Step 6: Once you've transversed the hole in one direction, rotate your sock by a quarter turn and weave over and under your original stitches until the hole (and the ½-inch ring around it) is patched in a basket weave.

Step 7: Snip off the end of the yarn (no knots under your tootsies!), right your sock, slip it on, wiggle your toes, and imagine a little tinkling sound. They're so, so happy right now!

More Nifty Tips

- For easier threading, hold the needle in your right hand, wrap one end of the yarn around the eye of the needle, and pinch the ends of the yarn together, holding the yarn taut with your left forefinger and thumb. Slide out the needle with your right hand, press the eye over the pinched yarn in your left hand, and pull through. Voilà!

- You can even go a little crazy by using one color of thread to stitch in one direction and another to stitch in the other. Ponder that magnificence for a minute or two!

- For lighter-weight socks, use embroidery thread rather than yarn.

Tie One On

. . .

"Buy things that will last and that are classic. Don't go in for all the fads. If you have a basic dress, put pretty jewelry with it or a scarf. You can change it. It could look different each time."
—BEATRICE NEIDORF

HOW TO KNOT A WINTER SCARF

The Classic Knot (for Warmer Days or Dress-Down Duds)

Step 1: Drape your scarf around your neck, pulling both ends even.

Step 2: Make a simple knot. Cross one end over the other, pull it up through the neck hole, and let it hang so it drapes nicely. Yes, it's easy, but sometimes less is more.

The Wrap Around (for Chilly Days or Chilling-Out Outfits)

Step 1: Drape your scarf around your neck, leaving the left side about a foot longer than the right.

Step 2: Reaching across your body with your right hand, grab the longer, left side of the scarf, loop it around your neck, and drape it across the right tail. Repeat, for added warmth.

The Parisian Knot (for Arctic Days or Hot Fashion)

Step 1: Fold your scarf in half lengthwise and drape it around your neck.

Step 2: Pull the loose ends through the loop on the other side. Ooh-la-la!

More Nifty Tips

• Use a scarf to add warmth *and* texture to any outfit. Try pairing a wooly number with a sleek, leather jacket or a silk one with a woven coat.

Get Crafty

...

"If there was absolutely no hope for mending something, it might end up as a dust rag. We never threw anything away."
—ALICE LOFT

HOW TO MAKE AN APRON

Step 1: Find a cute, old pillowcase that you no longer use (preferably one without drool stains or a Scooby-Doo pattern), and cut it in half width-wise. The open-ended side will serve as the body of your apron. Set it aside.

Step 2: Lay the close-ended half of your pillowcase flat and cut it in half again in the same direction. You'll end up with two more pieces: one closed at the end and one open on both sides. Set aside the close-ended piece. You can use it later to make pockets, if you'd like, or just to dust around your house.

Step 3: Lay the open-ended piece flat, and cut it in half once more in the same direction. You'll end up with two skinny loops. Snip each along one short seam, so you're left with two really long, thin strips of material. They'll be your apron ties.

Step 4: Match up your apron tie strips, right side to right side, and sew one short end together with a double-threaded needle to make one super-long tie. Here's how to do a simple (but strong) back stitch: Push your needle down through one side of the fabric and bring it back through the front a few millimeters ahead. Push your needle back down through your first hole and push it back through the front a few millimeters ahead of your second stitch. Press your needle down through your second stitch and back through the front a few millimeters ahead of your third, and repeat, leapfrogging your way along. Once you get to the end, make a couple of stitches in the same spot, pass your needle through the loop of thread, and snip.

Step 5: Lay your now super-long apron tie flat, right side down, and center on it your apron's body, or the open-ended half of the pillowcase. The raw-cut end of your apron should be on the tie and your bordered (or nicely sewn) end should be on the bottom.

Step 6: Fold the tie in half over the edge of the apron and, tucking the raw edges underneath, pin it in place. Continue folding, tucking, and pinning the entire length of the apron tie and, starting at one end, sew it together with a double-threaded needle using the same back stitch method. Don't forget to sew the tie ends closed, too! If you're feeling ambitious, run a back stitch along the closed side of the apron tie for a more finished look.

Step 7: Try it on, and get inspired! Now is the perfect time to bake a pie! Hmm, funny how that's *always* the case.

More Nifty Tips

- For a longer apron, simply adjust your cut in step 1 so the open-ended side of the pillowcase is your desired apron length.

- If you'd like to add pockets, cut off the corners of the close-ended piece of the pillowcase you set aside in step 2. Tuck, pin, and sew the raw edges together. Then pin the pockets to your apron and sew on three sides, leaving the top open. If you want

to get super fancy, use leftover material to make flaps or just add a colorful button on top of each pocket.

- No old pillowcases? Then improvise. You can make aprons from almost anything, including old dish towels, sheets, or tablecloths. Be creative!

Make A Mends

· · ·

"My mother's sister was a fantastic seamstress. She made clothes to drive you crazy!"
—RUTH ROWEN

HOW TO PATCH A HOLE

Step 1: Round up your supplies: a needle and thread, scissors, a ruler, and an iron, which you might as well turn on now. Also, choose some material to use as a patch. Decide whether you want it to blend in or make a statement. If you're an earth child, choose floral material. If you're a punk rocker, try zebra print. If you're a Journey fan, skip the patch altogether.

Step 2: Measure your hole, add an inch to each side, and then measure and cut your patch, using that larger magic number. So, for example, if your hole is 2 inches by 2 inches, cut a 3-inch by 3-inch patch.

Step 3: Lay your patch, facedown, on your ironing board (or on a thick towel on a table or floor). Fold each edge inward by ¼ inch. (If you have a seam gauge handy, it'll make measuring easier.) Then iron in the crease to make nice edges.

Step 4: Lay your patch on top of your hole, and fasten it in place with straight pins, placed parallel to the patch's edge.

Step 5: Measure two arm's lengths or so of thread, pass it through your needle, even up the ends, and tie them off together in a knot. Say, "Oh, not again!" and then, yes, knot again. Snip the excess.

Step 6: Place your hand inside the garment—say, the leg of your pants or arm of your jacket—so you don't accidentally go through the other side and sew it closed. Press your needle up from underneath the corner of your patch (not through your clothes) and pull it up and through to hide your knot.

Step 7: Just like you did when you were hemming (see page 98), now pass your needle through a few threads of your garment, as close to the patch's edge as possible, and then up through the bottom of the patch, making a stitch about every ¼ inch.

Step 8: After every third completed stitch, lock your work by passing your needle and thread once more through the patch only before continuing. (That way, if your patch catches on something, it'll be less likely to come completely loose.)

Step 9: On the final stitch, pass your needle through the resulting loop of thread before pulling it tight. Repeat three times and snip. You're good to go!

More Nifty Tips

- The best patches are those of similar density and texture to the fabric you're repairing. This probably doesn't need to be said, but just for good measure: Unless you're in a total jam, don't, say, sew a denim patch onto wool pants or a dainty silk patch onto jeans.

- Choose a thread to match your patch for best camouflaging.

- If you have a piece of fabric you love and can't seem to part with, save it for a patch!

Omit Oopsies

. . .

"Oh yes, we used boiling water for fruit stains. I'm still doing that. I'm still teaching it to people. And it works! It still works!"
—LUCILE FRISBEE

HOW TO REMOVE MOST STAINS

Grease, Red Wine, or Coffee

Step 1: Mix ¼ cup white vinegar with ¼ cup cold water. Stir in 1 teaspoon laundry detergent.

Step 2: Apply the solution to the stain and dab with a paper towel.

Step 3: Rinse with cold water.

Blood

Step 1: Assess whether or not you are bleeding at the moment. If so, forget your clothes and get help. If not, proceed.

Step 2: Mix 1 teaspoon mild laundry detergent and ½ teaspoon clear ammonia in ½ cup ice-cold water.

Step 3: Dab with a paper towel and rinse with cold water.

Step 4: If it persists, add 1 cup salt to 2 quarts cold water and soak the garment in it.

Berries

Step 1: Bring a kettle of water to a boil.

Step 2: Spread your stained clothing over the top of a bucket.

Step 3: Stand back and, holding the kettle a foot above the bucket, pour the boiling water through your stain. The heat, coupled with the force, should drive any reds or purples straight into the bucket.

Ink (Water-Based)

Step 1: Squeeze a lemon onto the stain.

Step 2: Set your garment out in the sunshine.

Step 3: Repeat as necessary.

Lipstick

Step 1: Examine the lipstick if it's not on your own shirt. Is it the same color you wear? Better be!

Step 2: Apply the teeniest bit of clear petroleum jelly on the spot, and dab it with a paper towel.

Step 3: Rinse it with mineral spirits or, if color-safe, hydrogen peroxide.

Mud

Step 1: Allow the mud to dry and then gently scrape as much of it off as you can.

Step 2: Apply rubbing alcohol (or denatured alcohol) to the dirt stain, and dab with a paper towel.

More Nifty Tips

• When in doubt, soak in cold water.

• Need some bleaching? Try sunshine first. It's free, it's cheerful, and it can often whiten better than any bleach.

Polish Your Image

• • •

"I wanted my shoes to be polished, because that made me feel good. Shiny shoes and clean clothes were the only things that could make us feel proud."
—ELOUISE BRUCE

HOW TO SHINE YOUR SHOES

Step 1: Wipe down your shoes, especially the heels and soles, with a soft, cotton cloth to remove all dust and dirt.

Step 2: Wrap a soft, cotton rag or old sock (ahem, a clean one) around your index and middle fingers.

Step 3: Dip your rag into a cup of room-temperature water, dab it into your shoe polish, and dip it back into the water. It should be damp, not soaking.

Step 4: Placing your opposite hand into your shoe for stability, start applying polish, tip to heel, using a tiny circular motion. Make several passes over the same small area before moving to the next.

Step 5: After polishing the entire shoe, dampen a clean cloth and make one even pass over the shoe to prevent drops or streaks.

Step 6: Allow the shoe to dry for 10 minutes.

Step 7: Buff both sides of the shoe with a horse hair polishing brush or a buffing cloth. (If you have neither, a pair of panty hose works surprisingly well.)

Step 8: To enhance the shine, from a seated position, place a shoe between your knees and, holding panty hose or a buffing cloth with both hands, slide it back and forth over the toe. To be super cool, snap the cloth. (Warning: The snap doesn't work so well with panty hose.)

More Nifty Tips

- If you get rock salt on leather shoes, add a tablespoon of vinegar to a cup of water, soak a cotton ball or paper towel, and gently wipe the salt away. Allow the leather to dry before polishing.

- Buff scuffs with a dab of non-gel, non-whitening toothpaste and a moist rag. Wipe clean.

Be Seamly

• • •

"I can still remember my first bought dress. I was ten years old.
It was cotton and it had a fine green spring print on it and a drop waist.
I felt pretty special."
—ALICE LOFT

HOW TO BUY QUALITY CLOTHING

Step 1: Take a deep breath before you rush to the cash register. However magnificent the sale or fancy the label, you want your clothing to last more than just a few wears.

Step 2: Give the garment a once-over, eyeballing for any holes, tears, or stains.

Step 3: Eyeball the material. If it's textured or patterned fabric, make sure the grain and design match up on each side of the seam.

Step 4: Give it a gentle tug. If the seams hold and the garment returns to its original shape, keep going. If it rips or morphs, put it back, slip your hands into your pockets, and slink away, whistling softly. Try not to let your eyes bug out of your head. They're a dead giveaway.

Step 5: Peek inside to check out the seams. They should be straight, not crooked, and the edges of material should be finished, not raw. If it looks like a child cut the pattern with a pair of garden shears, that's probably true. Put down the garment and immediately send money to some anti-sweatshop charity (see page 222 on how to afford charitable giving).

Step 6: Check out the fasteners. Try the zipper. Tug any hooks. Buttons should be secure and able to fit into the appropriate button holes. (Make sure they do, and make sure the holes are finished, not just cheapo slits in the fabric.)

Step 7: Try it on. Well-made garments just fit better, and you'll get much more wear out of something that flatters your figure.

Step 8: Put it on hold, and take a walk. If you still want it, need it, and can afford it, make the purchase, confident that you're buying quality.

More Nifty Tips

- If there's a lining inside, make sure it hangs straight and allows for some give.
- Check the length of the hem to ensure that any necessary alterations are possible.

Get on a Roll

. . .

*"You didn't give your clothes away. You packed them away in the attic.
So, when I got to be fourteen, I plundered the attic and reclaimed my
mother and aunt's old clothes. They had velvets and sateens. I remember
an elegant chiffon-sleeved dress, which I got down for myself."*
— Mildred Kalish

How to Pack a Suitcase

Step 1: Check the weather of your destination, and know your
itinerary.

Step 2: Set out your wish list. On your bed, gather all the clothes
you'd like to bring with you. Don't forget undies, socks, a bathing
suit, PJs, a belt, a going-out outfit, and a couple of sweaters to layer
if a chill sets in. Assuming you'll wear your comfy shoes to travel, include at most one or two more pairs (e.g., sandals and going-out
shoes). Then ogle your handiwork for a minute and take a deep
breath, knowing you won't really have to carry all that you see.

Step 3: Thin the pack. Ruthlessly, put each piece, with the exception of your undies, socks, and favorite going-out dress, to the mix-
and-match test. If any item can be worn only as part of a single
outfit, put it back in your closet. You can wear it again when you get
home.

Step 4: Place all of your toiletries in a plastic bag and lay it in the
bottom of your suitcase. Note: If you plan to carry your suitcase

onto an airplane, place your toiletries in a 1-quart plastic bag (with no more than 3 ounces of liquid per container) and carry it in your purse until you pass through security.

Step 5: Fold each of your pants in half lengthwise and stack them on top of each other from most wrinkle prone (on the bottom) to least (on top). Starting at the bottom of your pants, roll them together, until they form a tight cylinder. Place the roll, seam-side down, in your suitcase. Repeat process with any T-shirts, tanks, or sundresses.

Step 6: Fold any dressy shirts or jackets and lay them flat on top of your rolls.

Step 7: Stuff your shoes with socks and any other small accessories, like belts, film, or batteries. Then place your shoes in a plastic bag and lay them on top.

Step 8: Roll your undies and tuck them into any remaining available space, preferably not in your shoes.

Step 9: Zip it up and happy trails!

More Nifty Tips

- Wear your bulkiest clothes and shoes when traveling to save space in your suitcase.

- Always pack *less* than you think you should. You'll probably end up wearing your same favorite jeans or dress on most days anyway. And you shouldn't be saddled with stuff when you're out exploring the world.

- If you don't plan to unpack upon arrival at your destination and instead you plan to live out of your suitcase, consider rolling individual outfits together instead of pants with pants and shirts with shirts. That way, you can just pull out one roll at a time without making a mess.

- When in doubt, pack neutral-colored solids rather than patterns so you can mix and match more easily. Too boring? Spruce it up with accessories.

- If you plan to bring home any souvenirs, pack a small, empty duffel. You can fill it up and carry it with you on the way home.

- Avoid packing valuables, and stow any cheapo jewelry in a tiny ziplock pouch in your shoes. Leave the necklace clasp out of the bag to prevent knotting.

Nesting

. . .

Take pride in your surroundings.
Use your imagination,
and make your house a home.

Get Stoked

● ● ●

"We had a big cooking stove, which heated the kitchen and living room. It kept us warm by fire. You'd keep stoking it if you needed to keep it going or you'd let it go if you wanted it to go out."

—ALICE LOFT

HOW TO BUILD A FIRE

Step 1: Gather your supplies: some long wooden matches, a few broad sheets of newspaper (preferably pages you've already read), some skinny sticks (aka tinder), some huskier branches (aka kindling), and two or three dry, split, seasoned logs about 12 to 18 inches long. Optional (though highly suggested): a bag of marshmallows and a long stick on which to toast them.

Step 2: Ball up a few sheets of newspaper, and place them in your fire pit. Don't crumple them too tightly, or oxygen won't have room to circulate and your fire will fizzle.

Step 3: Stand your tinder on end to form a pyramid over the newspaper.

Step 4: Gently lay three to five pieces of kindling against or atop your structure.

Step 5: Without toppling or smothering your beautiful structure, carefully lay a couple of logs on top.

Step 6: Summon your inner pyromaniac (it will likely not be difficult), strike a match, and, starting in the back of the pile, light the paper's bottom-most edges in several places.

Step 7: Rub your hands together, and then hold them toward the fire to get toasty. Turn around and push your bottom closer. It'll feel even warmer if you give it a little shake.

More Nifty Tips

- If you're building your blaze in a fireplace, don't forget to open the damper first or your home will fill with smoke! If you feel cold air whooshing down your flue, light a piece of newspaper and hold it toward the back of your firebox. As the air heats up, it'll begin to rise and fight back the wind.

- Hardwoods, like oak, birch, cherry, and maple, burn longer, hotter, and cleaner than resin-heavy soft woods like pine or spruce, which can also increase your risk of chimney fire.

- Logs aged for 6 months to a year burn best. Newer, greener wood has more moisture, which means more smoke and a higher risk of chimney fire. To identify seasoned logs, look for lightweight wood with cracked and often darkened ends. Bat two pieces together. If your hear a *clunk*, it's ready to burn. If you hear a *thud*, it's still too new.

Stay Toasty

· · ·

"My mother knitted us scarves and mittens. They were much warmer than any you could buy. I even still have some of them."
— GRACE FORTUNATO

HOW TO KNIT A SCARF

Step 1: Choose your yarn, considering its material (wool is toasty but alpaca is as soft as all get out), color (you can never go wrong with red), and bulkiness (the fatter the yarn, the quicker the knitting). You'll also need some needles. Just check the yarn's label for the recommended gauge (or thickness) of the needle. The chunkier the needle, the faster the work.

Step 2: Take a deep breath and follow each of these steps bit by bit. Knitting can sound complicated, but you'll pick it up very quickly. For a great video tutorial, visit KnittingHelp.com.

Step 3: To cast on (or get started), hold your left hand out, palm down, as if you were about to shoot someone with your finger, and drape the tail end of the yarn over your thumb and the ball end of the yarn over your index finger. Secure both ends against your palm with the remaining fingers of your left hand. Holding a needle in your right hand, poke the tip through your fingers into the loop and press the yarn against your needle with your right index finger. Pull the yarn down toward the palm of your hand to form two loops (one over your thumb and one over your index finger). Swoop the tip of your needle up along the outside of your left thumb to come up through the thumb loop. Keeping the thumb loop on your needle, move the tip of the needle over to your right loop, press it down through the top of it, pull it back through your now-giant thumb loop, and let the yarn slip off your thumb. Pull your needle toward you to tighten the stitch (not too snug!), slip your thumb back underneath the yarn to resume your starting position, and repeat until your scarf is as wide as you'd like it to be. Count your stitches. You'll probably have somewhere between 12 and 25.

Step 4: Get ready to knit! Hold the stitch-covered needle in your left hand with the loops on the left side. Poke your left index finger under the yarn and wrap it once around. Then, keeping your index finger extended, grasp the needle between your thumb and your middle, ring, and pinky fingers. Poke the tip of your right needle through the front of the outermost loop on the tip of your left needle. Using your right index finger, gently hold the loop against your right needle. (You'll know you've done it right if the tips of your needles cross, with the left needle on top of the right and the tail of yarn out the left.) Dip the tip of your right needle underneath the new yarn, pull it through the loop, and slide the stitch off the left needle. (You'll now have a new loop on your right needle.) Repeat until you reach the end of the row. Check your work by counting the number of stitches now on your right needle. If you get the same number of stitches that you cast on, you've done it right. Move the needle with your finished stitches to your left hand and repeat until your scarf reaches the desired length.

Step 5: To finish your scarf (or to bind off), you'll play a game of leapfrog with your yarn. After you knit the first two stitches of your last row, use the tip of your left needle (or your fingers) to pick up the first stitch off your right needle, leap it over your second, and pull it off the tip. Then knit one more stitch, pick up the first, leap over your most recent stitch, and slip it off the end. Repeat until you bind off the entire row.

Step 6: Using a large yarn needle, hide the dangling tails at both ends of your scarf by weaving them through your stitches.

Step 7: Roll the scarf up, wrap it in paper, attach a big bow, and give it to a loved one. There may be no better gift in the world than a hand-knit scarf!

More Nifty Tips

• Use thick-and-thin yarn for your first project. Its varied texture helps hide any mistakes.

• Go slow to start. It'll become second nature in no time!

• If you poop out early, either set aside your project for later or cast off and congratulate yourself for making one amazing pot holder.

Be a Material Girl

• • •

"My grandmother handed down a couple of quilts that we wore to shreds.
They just got handed down until they were threadbare, and even then,
we'd use them in the summertime."

—ALICE LOFT

HOW TO MAKE A CRAZY QUILT

Step 1: Gather your supplies: a basket's worth of fabric scraps (of
any size or material), a stack of 12-inch squares of muslin (you'll need
12 blocks for a 3-foot by 4-foot baby quilt, 40 for a 5-foot by 8-foot
twin quilt, 72 for an 8-foot by 9-foot full or queen-sized quilt), backing and batting the size of your quilt, a measuring tape, straight pins,
a quilting needle, quilting thread, a thimble, an embroidery needle,
embroidery thread, crocheting thread, and scissors.

Step 2: Thread your needle, matching the ends of your thread at
the bottom. Knot off the thread end-to-end at the bottom, and then
start building your quilt, block by block. Crazy quilts are insanely
beautiful because they follow no pattern. You can just make it up as
you go! Start by placing one fabric scrap, right side up, in the center
of a muslin block. Then place a second scrap, right side down, on
top of the first, lining them up along one edge, and pin. (The fabrics
can be different sizes and shapes, so long as they share one border.)
Sew along this common edge (through both pieces of fabric and the
muslin). Snip and knot your thread, and flip the top piece of fabric
over. Next, take a third piece of fabric, big enough to connect to the
first two pieces along a common edge, and place it, right side down,

on top of the other pieces. Sew the common edge, trim off any excess (more than ¼ inch), and flip. Repeat until you have the whole square covered. As you work, you'll notice that each square will become easier to complete. Be patient. It may take you days (or even weeks) to finish all of your squares, so have fun with it. Put on some music, invite some friends over to help you, pour some wine (or put the crazy in crazy quilt and make margaritas). Whatever floats your boat!

Step 3: Make it last and make it fancy. Now that your fabric is attached to the muslin squares with simple stitches, it's time to really secure it and add a bit of flair. Thread an embroidery needle with whatever color of embroidery thread you like, and stitch over each seam. For a basic cross-stitch, sew diagonally along the seam in one direction and then return in the opposite direction to "x" each stitch. Once you master that, you can get creative. Some crazy quilters embroider flowers, leaves, feathers, you name it, to secure their fabrics. Feel free to experiment! Go wild! Let your crazy quilt live up to its name!

Step 4: Now that you have all of your crazy blocks finished, it's time to sew them together. Select two squares you'd like to live next to each other and match them right side to right side. A quarter of an inch from the edge, sew them up with a double-threaded needle. Repeat, until all of your squares are connected. For a 12-patch baby quilt, make three rows of four. For a twin, make five rows of eight. For a full or queen, make eight rows of nine.

Step 5: Wash and iron the backing fabric, and lay it flat, right side down. For a warmer, winter quilt, add a layer of batting (or even an old cotton blanket) on top. Lay your finished quilt on top, right side up.

Step 6. Line up each side, fold the top and bottom layers inward by ¼ inch, then pin and sew together with a double-threaded needle.

Step 7: Tie off your quilt. To connect the front and back pieces, double thread a needle with heavy-duty crocheting thread (no knot). On the corner (or in the center) of every patch, dip your needle through the front of the quilt and out the back, leaving a 2-inch tail in the front. Move your needle over ¼ inch and push it through the back and out the front. Repeat three or four times, snip your thread, and double-knot the ends together on the front of your quilt. Woo-hoo! All done! Now, pull it over your bed and take a long nap!

More Nifty Tips

- To get extra fancy, sew a button on top of each tie, or pull a ribbon through.

- To learn more embroidery stitches, and find retro-cool patterns, visit SublimeStitching.com.

- Remember that there is no one way to make a crazy quilt. In fact, it's the "imperfections" that make crazy quilts truly original.

Nail It

. . .

"When decorating your house, do what's comfortable. Do what you like. If you love pictures, use 'em. If you don't, don't. Just do what feels good!"
—RUTH ROWEN

HOW TO HANG A PICTURE

Step 1: Find the perfect spot. If you want to hang it in the dead center of the wall, measure the width of the wall and divide it in half. Mark the spot with a short vertical line (in pencil).

Step 2: Measure up. Pictures should hang at eye level, so unless you come from an unusually tall or short family, that means the center of the work should sit about 57 inches above the floor. Mark that height (along your vertical line) with a horizontal line to form a "t."

Step 3: Hold the center of your picture over that spot, and make a second horizontal line at the point where the top of your frame hits the wall.

Step 4: Flip your picture over to get a good look at its backside. If it has a hook, measure down from the top of the frame to the top of the hook. If it has a wire, pull it taut, and then measure down from the top of the frame to its peak.

Step 5: On your wall again, measure down (along your vertical center line) from your top-of-the-frame mark to the point where your wire or hook sits. Mark that point with a horizontal line and circle it. That's where your nail (or if you have a heavy frame, the bottom of your picture-hanging hook) will go.

Step 6: Tap on the wall on your magic spot.

- Does it make a dull *thud*? If so, lucky you! That means there's a stud beneath it. (No, not *that* kind. A wooden two-by-four.) Your next step: On your mark, tap in a nail at a 45-degree angle.

- Does the wall sound hollow? Then, not-quite-as-lucky you! You'll need either a picture-hanging hook based on the weight of your piece (the heavier your painting, the bigger the hook) or a hollow wall anchor and a screw. (If you don't use either, your picture will most certainly fall.) To use the hook, align the bottom of the "J" with your mark and tap in the nail. To use an anchor, predrill a hole, tap or screw in the anchor, and drive in the screw, leaving just enough room to hang the picture.

Step 7: Hang your picture, level it off, and marvel at your handiwork. Now, walk past the picture and see if its eyes are following you. If so, run!

More Nifty Tips

• If you're not sure if there's a stud beneath your wall, use a stud finder or look for screw dimples in the drywall.

• If you're hanging a light wire-backed picture from a nail, try this shortcut to eyeball the perfect spot: Put a nail through the bottom of an old yardstick. (Drill a hole first to make sure the wood doesn't crack.) Hang the picture from that nail, hold the yardstick-and-picture up to the wall where you'd like to see the picture. When you've found the right spot, tap the yardstick, so the nail marks it. Remove the picture, nail it for real, and hang it up.

Find Comfort

. . .

"I slept with my sisters. The four of us would share one bed. We didn't
sleep too much. I'll tell you that."
—ELOUISE BRUCE

HOW TO MAKE A PILLOW

Step 1: Choose your fabric. You can pretty much use any material you like, even scraps, so long as it passes the cheek test. Brush it gently on your face. Is it soft? Does it itch? Will it leave strange indentations on your skin if you fall asleep on it? Will a little drool ruin it? Will a lot of drool ruin it?

Step 2: Size it up. Decide how big you'd like your pillow to be, add an inch to each side, turn your fabric upside down, mark your measurements in chalk or pencil, and double-check them. Cut with sharp scissors. Repeat.

Step 3: Place your squares, right side to right side, so the wrong side of the material is facing you. (Your pillow-to-be should be inside out.) Fasten three sides with straight pins, which should run perpendicular to the edges of the fabric.

Step 4: By hand or machine, sew together all three sides and half of the fourth side, leaving about ½ inch between your seams and the edges of the material. Remove the pins, or—ouch!—you'll get pricked.

Step 5: Turn the material right side out and stuff with fiberfill, goose down, last year's crumpled tax returns, whatever you'd like.

Step 6: Fold the open edge inward, pin together, and sew shut. Celebrate your pillow with a nice long nap!

More Nifty Tips

- Add dried lavender when filling for a sweet, sleep-inducing scent.

- If you choose a patterned material, make sure your patterns match before cutting your fabric.

Stay Buff

. . .

"If you were lucky and you hit it just right, you'd buy a rug or maybe two small ones. They protected your floors, but even more so, they showed off your wherewithal. Only fairly well-off people had rugs."
—RUTH ROWEN

HOW TO REMOVE SCUFFS FROM HARDWOOD FLOORS

Step 1: Grab the offending honey, child, or four-legged friend. They probably made the scuff, so they better help buff it. This is clean family fun at its most literal.

Step 2: Check the finish of your floor, if you don't already know it off the top of your head. Go to a corner and press your fingernail along the wood. Do you see a soft residue? If so, your floor is coated in wax. Is it hard as a rock? Then your floor is coated with polyurethane.

Step 2: On waxed floors, buff the scuff with extra-fine steel wool (000) and solvent-based liquid hardwood floor cleaner. Then wipe clean with a dry towel and rewax. On polyurethaned floors, restore the shine by vigorously rubbing the scuff with a paper towel, old stockings, a tennis ball, or a dryer sheet. Voilà!

More Nifty Tips

- Prevent most scuffs and scratches by placing a doormat at your entryway. It'll help brush dirt off the bottom of your shoes, which, if tracked into the house, may damage your floors. Better yet, kick off your shoes as soon as you get home.

- Stick felt pads underneath all of your furniture legs to prevent scratches.

- For squeaky wax floors, apply more wax to the loud board. For squeaky polyurethaned floors, sprinkle talcum powder into the offending gap.

Bloom On

· · ·

"I just brought in some flowers. I'm going out to supper and I wanted to take some to the hostess. I got some for me, too! I love flowers. I'm not a good gardener, but I love to have them around."
—Sue Westheimer Ransohoff

How to Make a Centerpiece

Step 1: Wake up early. While your coffee is brewing, fill a plastic pail with lukewarm water; grab a sharp knife, shears, or clippers; and walk out to your garden. Collecting flowers in the early morning, when the stems are fully hydrated and the blooms and leaves are dewy, is the key to a healthy, long-lasting arrangement. A note of warning: No matter how beautiful your neighbor's garden is, stay on your own side of the hedge. Stolen flowers don't smell nearly as sweet.

Step 2: Select your harvest. If the bloom grows on a single stem, like a sunflower or dahlia, make sure it's fully open before you snip it. (Otherwise it may not open at all once you get it inside.) If a bunch of flowers grow along a single stem, like lilacs or snapdragons, make sure at least one flower or cluster is beginning to open and all are in full color.

Step 3: Make the cut. Holding your shears at a 45-degree angle, clip the stem about an inch from its bottom and immediately put the flower in your bucket. Repeat until you have as many flowers as you'd like. Don't feel bad about cutting them either. Trimming your flowers every once in a while helps your plants produce more blooms.

Step 4: Bring your flowers inside and select your vase(s). You can use anything from old milk bottles and mason jars to cups or out-of-use watering cans.

Step 5: Fill your pitchers with some homemade flower preservative. Mix 1 quart lukewarm water either with 1 teaspoon each of sugar and bleach and 2 teaspoons lemon juice; or with 2 teaspoons each of sugar and white vinegar. The only exception: Droop-prone flowers, like tulips and irises, prefer cold water to lukewarm water.

Step 6: Groom your stems. You never want your flowers to stand more than a third taller than your vase, or your arrangement may tip, so shorten them as necessary. Strip away any leaves that will sit underwater. Then, encourage them to drink by following these snipping rules:

For regular stems, cut at a 45-degree angle. For woody stems, like roses and lilacs, split the bottom inch of the stem by making a vertical cut into it. (Never smash.) Trim hollow-stemmed flowers, like delphiniums and Gerber daisies, straight across, then flip them upside down, fill them with water, cover the bottom with your thumb, plunk them in your water-filled vase, and then remove your thumb.

Step 7: Arrange your flowers on angles, working from the outside of the vase in, making sure it looks even from all sides. Finish with the center flower.

Step 8: Place your blooms where they'll bring you the most good cheer, but away from sunlight and drafts. Now, go see if your coffee is ready and enjoy your day!

More Nifty Tips

- Change your water at least every other day.

- When your blooms begin to wilt, cut them again and transfer to shorter vases.

- Don't overcrowd your flowers. If you have leftover blooms, put them in single vases throughout your house or, better yet, give them to a neighbor or someone you love.

Use Your Imagination

...

"We had a flower garden. We'd always clip bouquets. We still have bouquets. Flowers are important to decorate the house."
—Lucile Frisbee

How to Make Art out of Pressed Flowers

Step 1: Go to your garden on a sunny day around the early afternoon, after the dew has evaporated but before the blooms begin to close or the stems to droop. Choose the flowers you'd like to press, and snip them at the base. The flatter the blooms, the better. (Think pansies and violets, not peonies or zinnias.)

Step 2: Find and dust off your old phone book. Then trim your flowers' stems, spread your blossoms flat between the pages, and close the book. (If you don't have a phone book, lay your blossoms between two coffee filters and tuck into an encyclopedia, dictionary, or one of your Norton anthologies that you haven't opened since college.)

Step 3: Place more books (or any other heavy object) on top of your newly recruited flower press and let it be for one to two weeks.

Step 4: Check on your flowers. If they're papery and dry, they're finished. Handle them with care (and tweezers). They're oh-so-delicate.

Step 5: Using just a touch of glue, mount your blossoms on a piece of paper or matte. Place in a frame and hang on your wall (see page 133 for help).

More Nifty Tips

- You can also glue your flowers to plain cards, write sweet notes on the back, tuck in an envelope, and send to a friend.

- Press pretty leaves and, for luck, four-leaf clovers, too!

Breathe Deep

• • •

"Cinnamon is wonderful. It makes your house smell like
you're baking a pie."
—BEATRICE NEIDORF

HOW TO SCENT YOUR HOME WITHOUT CANDLES

Step 1: Put that $30 you were about to spend on a fancy candle
back in your pocket.

Step 2: Pour water into a small pot and place it on the stove over
low heat.

Step 3: Add several cinnamon sticks (or a few shakes of ground
cinnamon), and if you'd like, cloves and peels of a lemon, orange, or
apple.

Step 4: Let simmer for as long as you'd like, making sure there's
always water in the pan.

More Nifty Tips

- If the weather is warm, open your windows. Fresh air smells so
sweet!

- Had fish for dinner? Cracked a rotten egg? Forgot to take the
trash out? A bowl of white vinegar, set on the countertop, will
absorb the foul odors in the air.

Go with the Flow

...

"What a much better life it is when you can do things for yourself!"
—Sue Westheimer Ransohoff

How to Unclog a Drain

Step 1: Sprinkle ½ cup baking soda down your slow-running or clogged drain.

Step 2: Wash it down with ½ cup white vinegar. It'll bubble like your fifth-grade science experiment, but put the stopper over it and let the fizz work for 15 minutes.

Step 3: In the meantime, put on a full kettle to boil water.

Step 4: After your 15 minutes are up and your kettle whistles, unplug the drain and pour the boiling water down it. Repeat if necessary.

More Nifty Tips

• If that still doesn't work, fill your sink with several inches of water (if it's not—ew—already filled), plug your overflow holes with a wet rag, rim your plunger with petroleum jelly, place it over the drain, and press up and down on the handle until the obstruction clears.

- Sprinkle ½ cup baking soda down your drains weekly, followed by hot tap water, to keep them fresh and clear.

- Put a sink trap, or small screen, over your drain to prevent food or hair from being washed down it.

Cut the Crap

· · ·

"We always had a plunger. Otherwise, it was a plumber!"
—Grace Fortunato

How to Unclog a Toilet

Step 1: This is not going to be pretty, but there's no way around it. First, stop flushing. If the water is still rising, look for the handle on the wall behind the toilet and turn the water off.

Step 2: Assess your surroundings. Are you at a friend's house or is there someone sitting in your living room waiting for you? If not, lucky you! If so, holler out to your pal and ask her to put on some loud music. She may think you're a little weird, but that may be better than having her think about what you just did to clog the toilet. If you didn't already, you're going to make some noise in step 4.

Step 3: If the water is to the top of the bowl, find a bucket or paper cup or whatever you can and bail some of it out. Gross? Yes, but not as gross as having dirty toilet water splash all over the floor.

Step 4: Find the plunger, and place the suction cup end over the hole in the bottom of the toilet bowl. Once you've got a good seal, press that handle up and down like you've never pressed it before. Do it vigorously! Wipe the sweat off your brow, and repeat until the water drains. (That means the clog has cleared.) If you turned the water off, turn it back on now.

Step 5: Once you've got the all clear, flush to clean the bowl, wash your hands (with soap!), and walk out with your head held high, as if nothing at all interesting happened in there.

More Nifty Tips

- If the plunger doesn't do the trick after as many tries as your muscles will allow, you'll need to crank an auger, or snakelike wire, down the hole.

- For toilets, flange (or bell-shaped) plungers work better than ball (or half-dome shaped) plungers.

6

Thriving

...

A good life isn't about being fancy.
It's about being healthy,
taking care of yourself,
and being happy.

Soothe a Cold

• • •

"When I was sick, my mother would give me loads of orange juice and tea with lemon. The mere fact that I was being fussed over? That did it!"
—Ruth Rowen

How to Make a Hot Tea Toddy

Step 1: Brew a cup of tea by pouring boiling water over a tea bag, preferably a decaffeinated one so you don't get jittery. Let steep for a few minutes.

Step 2: Add a twirl of honey to taste. Not only will the sweet stuff make it taste good, but it'll also coat your throat to help relieve any soreness or coughing.

Step 3: Quarter a lemon and squeeze a piece over the cup to add some lip-smacking tartness.

Step 4: Add a shot of whiskey or bourbon to the tea. Depending on how bad you feel, add a shot of whiskey or bourbon to your mouth, too.

Step 5: Hold the cup to your face, breathing in the hot steam to clear your schnoz.

Step 6: Climb under your covers, and sip until you get drowsy.

Step 7: Set the glass down first. Very important! Then fall asleep.

Step 8: Dream good dreams. Snoring is optional. Don't be shy. You're sick; you're allowed to saw wood.

More Nifty Tips

• Sit fireside to stay toasty. Feeling chilled can suppress your immune system.

• Gargle warm water three times a day to help wash away germs.

• Wash your hands often with soap (no fancy antibacterial stuff required) and, for goodness sake, keep them away from your face.

Plant One On

· · ·

*"I still follow the same beauty regimen. I cut off the lower stem
of an aloe plant, peel it back about an inch with a sharp knife, and rub it
all over my face every morning. For an eighty-eight-year-old, my
skin is still not bad."*
—Mildred Kalish

How to Soothe a Minor Burn with a Plant

Step 1: Assess your burn. If it's serious, seek medical attention. If
it's not, then with clenched teeth and a pained smile, suck in a deep
and noisy breath, allowing the air to rush over your molars. This
won't help your injury at all, but it may earn you some sympathy
from anyone standing nearby.

Step 2: Break off a bottom leaf from an aloe plant, and watch the
clear, goopy sap begin to ooze.

Step 3: Smear the sap from the leaf onto your burn for cool comfort. It'll help reduce inflammation and redness.

Step 4: If sap remains inside the leaf, store the leaf in your freezer
to help maintain its freshness. Hopefully, you'll never need it again,
but if you do, you'll have it handy.

More Nifty Tips

- Fresh aloe also helps soothe sunburn and itches from insect bites and poison ivy.

- Even black-thumbed gardeners can grow aloe vera plants. They thrive indoors, in full or partial sun, and they require very little water.

Sniffle-Proof Your Allergy Season

•••

*"There were a lot of wildflowers growing along the road in
Iowa—goldenrods, bright blue cornflowers, and wild roses."*
—MILDRED KALISH

HOW TO EASE YOUR SNEEZES

Step 1: Check the weather. If it's a sunny, dry, and windy day,
close your windows, hunker down inside, and pretend you're a vam-
pire. You can go out at night, when the pollen settles down. Rainy
days have lower pollen counts, too, so if you're super-sneezy, consider investing in a pair of galoshes and running your errands on wet
days.

Step 2: When you do go out, kick off your shoes as soon as you
come home. Otherwise, you may track pollen all through your
house, which would be so irritating, both physically and emotion-
ally. Still sneezing? Rinse off and put on some fresh clothes.

Step 3: Postpone your laundry day—or dry your clothes in the
dryer. If you hang wet clothes on the line, they'll be covered in pollen
by the time you take them in and you'll surely suffer for it. Achoo!

More Nifty Tips

- If you let your dog or cat outside, wipe her down with a damp
  towel before she comes back in, or you may start sneezing at the
  very sight of her, thanks to her pollen-toting fur.

- Hire (or bribe) someone else to mow your lawn and haul away the clippings. For bartering ideas, see page 224.

- About a month before allergy season begins, have a nip of local honey every day. Because it has local pollen in it, some people believe that teensy doses may help you build up your tolerance. Even if they're wrong, it'll still sweeten your day.

Get Fit for Free

• • •

"If I'm not fit and healthy, I can't enjoy all that's waiting for me."
—Lucile Frisbee

How to Build a Walking Regimen

Step 1: You don't need a gym membership or any fancy kicks to go walking, but you do need some shoes that offer decent arch support, a good amount of cushion, and a flexible sole. In other words, don't hoof it in your cute ballet flats. Just tie on some comfy shoes and head outside.

Step 2: Get moving. You've been walking since you were a babe, so you're already a pro at it. Start with a 5-minute warm-up at an

easy-does-it pace. Then speed up a bit for 2 minutes. Recover at your easy pace for 1 minute. And repeat the sequence five times. Finish up with 5 minutes of strolling, and give yourself a pat on the back.

Step 3: Switch it up. To build your endurance and strength, you've got to change your routine. There are all sorts of things you can do each time you hit the pavement: Add a minute to each speedy bout but keep your recovery the same. Add another fast-slow round to the routine. Try a hillier route. Or invent your own intervals by choosing a landmark (e.g., the stop sign, the lamppost, the shirtless guy washing his Camaro) and alternating fast and slow bouts between them. Do whatever makes it fun!

Step 4: Keep it up. As long as you're moving 30 minutes a day most days a week, your heart will be strong, your muscles will be sculpted, and your energy will be boundless.

More Nifty Tips

- Make sure your shoes are big enough. Your dogs will swell from exercise, so allow a thumb's width of space between your toe and the tip of your shoe.

- To make each step easier, bend your elbows to 90 degrees and swing your arms front to back, not side to side. You're speed-walking, not sashaying.

- Push off from the ball of your back foot to add spring to your step. Squeezing your tush while you do so will give you added tone.

- Invite a friend along. Not only will you have more fun, but you'll also be more likely to stick with it.

- Didn't even break a sweat? Try alternating running and walking next time.

Get a Natural Glow

• • •

"Make the most of what you have and try to be happy with yourself.
Try not to be what you can't be."
—BEATRICE NEIDORF

HOW TO GIVE YOURSELF A FACIAL

Step 1: Put a kettle on, place four to six green tea bags in a pitcher, and pour the boiling water over them. Let it steep for several minutes, and then place your pitcher in the fridge to chill.

Step 2: Pull your hair back from your face with a headband or ponytail holder (or, if you want to pretend that you're Little Edie Beale for a few minutes, a turtleneck that you've only partially taken off).

Step 3: Wash your face with cleansing soap and lukewarm water. Pat dry with a clean towel.

Step 4: Apply a homemade mask, and wait 20 minutes. A few ideas:

For oily skin, beat together 2 egg whites and 1 yolk, paint it on your face with a brush, and let dry.

For dry skin, mix a squirt of honey with a few drops of lemon juice and massage the mask into your face with your fingertips.

For flakey skin, mix 1 cup oatmeal with water or plain yogurt to make a paste, apply it to your face, and gently scrub.

For any skin type, peel and slice ½ cucumber, add 1 tablespoon of plain yogurt, puree, and massage it into your face.

Step 5: Rinse your face, using the chilled green tea tonic you've already made.

Step 6: Apply moisturizer, check out your newly radiant skin, and carry that I-look-amazing feeling with you all day long.

More Nifty Tips

- Give yourself a facial massage as you apply each mask to brighten your skin. Move your fingertips in small circular motions, starting in the center of your chin and working your way along your jawline. Then move to the center of your forehead and work your way out. Finish around your eyes and along your nose.

- No green tea bags? Try chamomile. None of that either? Then, just use lukewarm water to rinse. It'll still feel great!

Take the Cake

...

*"Have a clean face. You'll look better without makeup than
most people look with it."*
—RUTH ROWEN

HOW TO REMOVE MAKEUP

Step 1: Pull your hair away from your face using a headband or
ponytail holder, and take a look at what you've got going on, you
fox. Ooh-la-la!

Step 2: Gently wipe off any lipstick with a piece of soft tissue.

Step 3: Uncover your sparkly eyes. If you're wearing mascara, eye
shadow, or eyeliner, dab a tiny bit of moisturizer (or even Vaseline)
onto your closed peepers and, with a cotton pad, rub gently to wipe
clean.

Step 4: Scrub-a-dub-dub. Wet your hands with lukewarm water,
and get a lather going with either a dime-sized squirt of liquid
cleanser or a few rubs of a gentle cleansing soap. Gently rub your
face in a circular motion for 60 seconds, working your way from
your hairline to your neck.

Step 5: Rinse. Splash your face with lukewarm water to remove
all the soap, and then with colder water to close your pores.

Step 6: Pat dry with a clean, dry towel.

Step 7: Get a natural glow. Apply your favorite moisturizer, check yourself out in the mirror, and then say, "Mirror, mirror on the wall, who's the fairest of them all?" Smile, get over yourself, and go to bed.

More Nifty Tips

- Only use makeup in moderation. It should enhance your features, not hide them.

- You don't have to spend a fortune on fancy eye makeup removers, soaps, cleansers, and moisturizers. Many beauty products, regardless of their price tags, share the same basic ingredients. Just find something that works for your skin, and stick with it.

- For even brighter skin, use a clean washcloth—instead of your hands—to apply the soap.

Be a Perfect 10

• • •

"Nail polish was very important. It made us feel dressed up. I remember asking my father which of two colors he thought was better. He really thought about it before giving me his answer."
—Sue Westheimer Ransohoff

How to Give Yourself a Manicure (or Pedicure)

Step 1: Remove any old nail polish, and clip your nails. If they're long enough that they impede you from, say, holding a pencil, buttoning a shirt, or dialing a phone, then make haste. Not sure if yours qualify as Dragon Lady nails? Then they obviously do. Stop reading, go get your clippers, and trim them now. You'll feel so liberated (and you'll be able to wear darker colors without looking like a dominatrix).

Step 2: File the sides straight, and then round the corners so the curve of your nails matches the curve of your cuticles.

Step 3: Rub some lotion into your cuticles, and then gently push them back, using a soft towel.

Step 4: Clean your nails with nail polish remover, whether or not they're painted. It'll help your polish last longer.

Step 5: Apply a base coat. The key for a smooth shine: Dip your brush once, then make a thick stripe in the center of your nail. Repeat on either side to finish the job in three quick brushes. Don't double-dip for one nail; otherwise your polish may pool.

Step 6: Wait a few minutes and add a second coat. Repeat once more with a top coat.

Step 7: Refrain from rocking out on your Les Paul, shuffling cards, playing the washboard, or doing any other vigorous hand-centric activity for an hour.

More Nifty Tips

- If your cuticles are a mess, massage oil (olive, almond, Wesson, whatever you've got) into any trouble spots and then exfoliate them with a buffer. Skip the scissors; you may just make them worse.

- Be bold in your color choices, especially on your toes. Nail polish isn't permanent, so why not take a chance on Paint My Moji-Toes Red or Yoga-ta Get This Blue? And unless you live in flip-flops, no one will see it except your honey.

Stand Tall

. . .

"Good posture is very important. Hold your head up high and look straight out at the world and say, 'Here I am!'"
—BEATRICE NEIDORF

HOW TO PERFECT YOUR POSTURE

Step 1: Stand with your feet shoulder-width apart, knees slightly bent, arms by your sides, and weight on the balls of your feet. Not only does standing tall help reduce injury and muscle fatigue, but it also boosts confidence. Seriously, try it.

Step 2: Draw your tummy in and upward, as if you'd like your belly button to kiss your spine. Smack!

Step 3: Keeping your chin level, gently press your shoulders down and back.

Step 4: Check your alignment in a mirror. From the front, your shoulders and hips should be level, your arms should hang equidistantly from your sides, your knees should face forward, and your ankles should be straight up and down. From the side view, you should be able to draw a straight line from your earlobes, through your shoulders, hips, knees, and ankles.

Step 5: Say the following two words: Hubba, hubba! You'll feel better (and people will treat you better) if you stand tall and carry yourself with confidence.

More Nifty Tips

- Don't wear high heels every day, or you could throw your back out of whack.

- To sit with perfect posture, place both feet flat on the floor, your toes pointing forward, your knees slightly behind your ankles, and your hips parallel to or slightly higher than your knees. Pulling your abs in and your shoulders back, sit against the back of the chair so your lower spine is supported.

- When sleeping on your side, place a pillow between your legs. When sleeping on your back, place a pillow under your knees.

Know Your Assets

· · ·

"I used to ask God, 'Would it have hurt to have made me a little prettier?' I thought I was fat, and I wasn't then and I'm not now. That's come as a huge surprise to me in my old age."
—MILDRED KALISH

HOW TO LOVE YOUR BODY AT ANY SIZE

Step 1: Find some perspective. In the grand scheme of things, whether or not you can fit into those size 0 jeans has absolutely nothing—zero! zippo! zilch!—to do with your value as a person. Hey, did you just roll your eyes? Then try this. Think of some women, past or present, whom you admire. Was Rosa Parks, the African American woman who refused to move to the back of the bus, a hero because of her dress size—or her courage? Is Ellen DeGeneres so beloved because of how tightly she can notch her belt—or how hard she can make us laugh? Has Hillary Clinton risen so high in government because of her waistline—or her brain? Ask yourself what you hope people will celebrate you for.

Step 2: Be physical. You only get one body to live in (and love) in this lifetime, so you might as well appreciate it. Rather than obsess about how you look, consider for a moment what you can *do*. Have your legs carried you to mountaintops? Have your arms offered comfort to friends who've needed hugs? Keep a gratitude journal, where you list all the cool things your body has helped you accomplish each week. Read it whenever you're feeling down.

Step 3: Surround yourself with positive people. Body hang-ups can be contagious. If you spend all your time with friends who disrespect their own bodies, you may begin to feel pressure to do the same with yours. Don't give in! Make it a policy among your peers to voice only positive body thoughts, and support each other in doing so. You'll see soon enough that it feels so good!

Step 4: Embrace your curves (or your lack thereof). Whatever you have, work it! There is no single definition of pretty or sexy or beautiful. It's up to you to define for yourself. Don't let anyone else do it for you.

More Nifty Tips

- Ban the negative self-talk. You'd never, *ever* tell a loved one that she looks too skinny or too fat, too tall or too short. Give yourself the same due respect.

- Toss your scale. Why give your power away to a number? If you're healthy and strong, that's all you need to know.

Get Refreshed

· · ·

*"It's a real joy, climbing into a bed that's been freshly made
with sundried sheets."*
—MILDRED KALISH

HOW TO GET A GOOD NIGHT'S SLEEP

Step 1: Rise and shine at the same time every day. That means no sleeping until 11 A.M. on Saturdays (unless you do it every other day, too, lazybones) and no hitting the snooze button seven times every morning. Establishing a regular A.M. routine will help calibrate your body's clock, making it easier to fall asleep at night.

Step 2: Exercise in the morning or afternoon, not the evening. People who work out sleep longer and better than those who don't. But because exercise makes you hot (literally *and* figuratively), you should allow three to six hours between your sweat and sleep sessions. In order to drift off, your body needs to chill out.

Step 3: Have dinner early, and skip the chicken vindaloo. Eating heavy or spicy meals within three hours of bedtime can disrupt sleep for reasons you can probably guess. (If you can't guess them, then turn to page 148 to prepare for the worst-case scenario.)

Step 4: Ritualize bedtime. Ease your mind into la-la land by doing something that relaxes you. Try: Taking a bath, listening to soothing music, reading, meditating. Skip: Paying bills, watching Fox News, looking up exes on the Internet.

Step 5: Climb into bed-di-bye. The darker and quieter your bedroom, the better. Sweet dreams!

More Nifty Tips

- Caffeine, nicotine, and booze all lead to restless nights, so go easy on all three.

- Most people prefer cooler temps for sleeping, so turn your thermostat down before you turn your bed down.

- Use your bed only for sleeping and nookie, never work or worry.

Feel Invincible

• • •

"It took me a long time to overcome my fears, but you have to do it."
—GRACE FORTUNATO

HOW TO PROTECT YOURSELF FROM DANGER

Step 1: Avoid trouble. Steer clear of bad guys (and wild animals) by using common sense. Close and lock your doors. Walk in well-lit, well-populated areas. Keep your eyes and ears open.

Step 2: Trust your gut. If something just doesn't feel right, remove yourself from the situation. It's absolutely not rude to walk—or run—away! (If it's a raccoon or other misguided wildlife we're talking about here, go to a neighbor's house, call animal control, and let them handle the rest. If not, proceed to step 3.)

Step 3: Make noise. If you're in trouble, attract as much attention to yourself as possible. Yell, shout, blow a whistle.

Step 4: If you can't get away or get help and you're being attacked, fight back using everything you've got. Not to sound too terribly grim, but punch, hit, kick, knee, bite, and scratch that troublemaker. If you've got coins in your pocket, throw them. Hair spray or pepper spray? Spray it! A frying pan on the stove top? Oh, you know what to do, darling.

Step 5: Run away as soon as you can and get help.

More Nifty Tips

- Making eye contact can thwart a bad situation because it helps demonstrate to shady characters that you're aware of your surroundings. It tells them you're the wrong girl to pick on.

- Switch up your daily patterns, so your whereabouts are unpredictable.

- If you plan to hit somebody (or something) with your cast-iron skillet, resist taking the bacon out of it first. Bacon is good, but not that good.

- If the troublemaker just wants your money (or iPod or jewelry), give it to him. Your safety is much more valuable than your possessions.

Feel Glamorous

· · ·

"We all started wearing lipstick by age twelve, because movie stars wore lipstick. Oh my, we were in heaven! If you had some on, that meant you were dressed."
—Mildred Kalish

How to Wear Red Lipstick

Step 1: Soften your kisser. Gently brush off any rough skin with a dry toothbrush or a damp washcloth. Don't pick or peel! You want your lips to be red from your lipstick, not gushing blood.

Step 2: Dry your lips. Blotting with a tissue will do the trick.

Step 3: Choose a liner the same shade as your lipstick, and line the edge of your mouth. It'll help prevent your color from bleeding. If you can't find an exact match, use a lighter shade. Never, ever go darker, lest you look like a televangelist's mistress.

Step 4: Starting at the center of your mouth and moving toward the corners of your lips, apply lipstick directly from the tube. Blot gently and repeat.

Step 5: Pucker up!

More Nifty Tips

- Accentuate only one feature at a time. If you're going for dramatic lips, keep your eyes and cheeks natural.

- Experiment with different shades of red. Warmer tones flatter yellower skin, while bluer shades look good on pinker complexions.

- Don't be afraid to mix shades to create your own custom color.

- Too dark? Blot or apply lip gloss on top to help lighten lips.

Loving

. . .

Take care of your family.
There is no better return on your investment.
Your love for them will make the bad times less painful
and the good times more joyous.

Calm Your Babe

. . .

*"Give your children respect and they have to respect you. Give them
privacy and also trust them. And try to set a good example. If you're a
good role model, they'll emulate what you're trying to do."*
—BEATRICE NEIDORF

HOW TO SWADDLE A NEWBORN BABY

Step 1: Spread a small blanket diagonally on a changing table or
bed.

Step 2: Fold the top corner down about 6 inches.

Step 3: Lay the baby on the blanket, so the fold is just above the
baby's shoulders and the bottom point is in line with his toes. Say
coochie-coo.

Step 4: Gently holding the baby's right arm to his side, pull the
same side of the blanket across the baby, tucking the corner beneath
his bottom.

Step 5: Leaving enough room for the baby's legs to extend, fold up the bottom point of the blanket toward the baby's chin. If the blanket is too long, fold the bottom point down so it's not covering the baby's face.

Step 6: Gently holding the baby's left arm to his side, pull the final corner of the blanket across him and tuck beneath his bottom.

Step 7: Pick him up and give him a sweet kiss.

More Nifty Tips

• If you've got a particularly wild baby, good luck! Leave his arms free by folding down the top corner farther and aligning the fold under his armpits. When you fold up the bottom corner, secure it by tucking it into the other folds at the top.

Spark Imagination

• • •

"You don't have to have toys with all the bells and whistles. It just takes a little imagination!"
—GRACE FORTUNATO

HOW TO MAKE A BABY TOY

A Cinchy-Inchy Caterpillar

Step 1: Dig out an old pair of brightly colored (ahem, clean) stockings, and snip off one leg about 15 inches above the toe.

Step 2: Stuff it with six pieces of crumpled paper, a baby fave for its noise and texture.

Step 3: Knot off the end of the stocking, and trim the excess.

Step 4: Cut five pieces of contrasting ribbon, in 8-inch lengths, and tie each segment around the stocking between each piece of paper. Secure each with a double knot.

Step 5: Name your bug-a-lug, and present it to your babe.

A Rolling Rattle

Step 1: Find a clean, empty coffee can.

Step 2: Fill it with noisemakers, like beans, rice, or acorns.

Step 3: Secure the can's lid. Some heavy-duty tape, like duct tape, or even a few drops of super glue will keep it in place.

Step 4: Wrap the canister in cheerful paper and securely tape the ends.

Step 5: Set the rattle on the floor next to your babe. She'll love to push it around, especially if she can crawl behind it.

More Nifty Tips

• Don't stress too much about making or buying the Perfect Baby Toy. Everything, even a cardboard box or a piece of paper, is new, and therefore stimulating. Besides, your baby will learn so much more from you than from anyone or anything else.

Make Sweet Dreams

• • •

"Reading your kids bedtime stories is a wonderful thing and so intimate. Do the voices. Just pretend you're on a stage acting. Don't make it dull and blah blah blah. You have to be animated, but not so animated that you'll wake them up."

—BEATRICE NEIDORF

HOW TO READ A BEDTIME STORY

Step 1: Allow your child to choose his favorite book. If he's having trouble deciding, give him a choice between two.

Step 2: Get cozy. Turn off all distractions, like the radio or television, dim the lights a bit (but not so dark that you strain your eyes), and tuck in your tyke, already washed, brushed, and dressed in pajamas.

Step 3: Make it fun. Position the book so the child can see the pictures, and begin reading aloud slowly, using different voices for each character, if you can swing it.

Step 4: Ask questions, preferably ones that don't have right or wrong answers. For example: What would you do? What do you think happens next? Do you have any friends like that? Make it an interactive experience, not a quiz.

Step 5: Kiss your child good night, tell him you love him, turn off the lights, and go relax.

More Nifty Tips

- Steer clear of any scary stories, especially right before bedtime, or a little one may be joining you in your bed after the lights go out.

- Stick with the same book a few nights in a row; it'll help your child develop his language skills more quickly.

- Join your local library (it's free!) and choose your bedtime stories together.

Send Some Love

. . .

"The most important part of being a good cook: You have to care about the person you're cooking for."
—Ruth Rowen

How to Pack a Lunch

Step 1: Peek inside your fridge. If you spot any leftovers from last night's dinner, just pack them up and, voilà, you're done.

Step 2: No leftovers? No problem. Just make a sandwich (with 3 ounces protein, 1 tablespoon fat, and lots of veggies) on whole wheat bread. Try turkey with lettuce, tomato, cheese, and mustard; or tuna with low-fat mayo and spinach; or peanut butter and jam with carrot sticks on the side. Pack the sammy in a washable reusable container or wrap it in aluminum foil (recyclable) or waxed paper (compostable).

Step 3: Choose a piece of fruit for dessert.

Step 4: Add a beverage to whet the whistle; pour 8 ounces skim milk or juice into a reusable thermos. Buying in bulk and using a thermos, rather than buying individual juice or milk boxes, will save money (and the earth).

Step 5: Toss all of it into a reusable lunch box or satchel.

Step 6: Slip in a sweet, handwritten note to show your love. Want to be a little less mushy? Try a joke. Here's one: Two snowmen are standing in a field. One says to the other, "Funny, I smell carrots, too!"

More Nifty Tips

- If the meal includes anything perishable, stash it in an insulated bag or box and add a cold pack (or a baggie filled with ice) to keep it cool.

- If mornings are hectic, pack it the night before and stow it in the fridge.

- The more (naturally) brightly colored the meal (think green spinach, red peppers, orange carrots, etc.), the more nutritious it's likely to be. Rainbows never tasted so great!

Teach Responsibility

· · ·

"I don't think children should be paid to do chores. I think they should do them as part of the family. It's everybody's job to keep going."
—Alice Loft

How to Delegate Chores

Step 1: Assess what needs to be done around the house. Unless you want to be relegated to the status of family maid, understand that running a household is a group endeavor. Be sure to explain this fact to everyone under your roof. Persist, even if moaning ensues.

Step 2: Make a chart for each family member, listing his chores down the side and the days of the week across the top.

Step 3: Be realistic. When assigning chores, consider which tasks your child will be able to complete successfully and may also, possibly, maybe, even just a little bit, actually enjoy. If necessary, demonstrate the proper way to perform the duty and observe your child's first attempt, offering plenty of encouragement along the way.

Step 4: Give a check mark (or star or smiley face) for each completed task.

Step 5: Review the chart at the end of each week to determine who has done their work.

Step 6: Establish consequences. Reward those who've successfully completed their tasks and eliminate privileges for those who haven't. And stick to it, despite any and all fits and wails. If you don't, the entire system will fall apart.

More Nifty Tips

- Start early. Even children as young as three or four can learn to contribute in simple ways by, say, picking up their toys, feeding the dog, or carrying cups to the sink.

- Reward your children with praise, not money, for pitching in, lest they consider taking care of themselves, and their family, an optional task. Gold stars? Fine. Gold bars? Not so much.

- Rotate chores on a weekly or monthly basis to help eliminate boredom and also to teach your child multiple skills.

Urge Action

• • •

HOW TO RAISE A GOOD CITIZEN

Step 1: Set a good example. Your children watch everything you do, so demonstrate kindness, generosity, and honesty every day. Say please and thank you, hold doors open for strangers, pick up trash on the sidewalk, and stop for a chat with a lonely neighbor.

Step 2: Volunteer together. Whether you're licking stamps at a campaign office, tending a community garden, or serving up food at a soup kitchen, bring your youngster along to help. Not only will she feel empowered, but she'll also learn empathy.

Step 3: Vote. Bring your child behind the curtain with you as you pull the lever, and explain to her the importance of having a voice.

More Nifty Tips

- Set up a lemonade stand, and have your child donate the profits in person to the charity of her choice.

- Allow your little one to gather her too-small clothes and deliver them, together, to a homeless shelter. She'll learn that even small actions can generate meaningful change.

Dress 'Em Up

· · ·

"My husband was firmly convinced that it was the job of the husband to do the most he could for his family, and he didn't want to be thanked. But I thanked him anyway."
— RUTH ROWEN

HOW TO TIE A NECKTIE

Step 1: Pop up your sweetie's collar, tell him how cute he looks, and then drape the tie around his neck with the wide end on your left (his right) and the narrow end on your right (his left).

Step 2: Gently tug the wide end down, so it hangs about 12 inches below the narrow end.

Step 3: Cross the wide end over the narrow end and bring it up through the neck loop and down the front.

Step 4: Swing the wide end to the right (toward his left shoulder), pass it under the narrow end to the left (toward his right shoulder), and then cross it over the narrow end to the right (toward his left shoulder, again).

Step 5: Pass the wide end up through the neck loop once more, tuck it through the knot, and let it hang down.

Step 6: Holding the narrow end with your left hand, scoot the tie knot up with your right hand toward your honey's neck to secure. Not too tight!

Step 7: Fold his collar down, adjust the knot once more, give him a smooch, and tell him how handsome he looks.

More Nifty Tips

- Always fasten the top button of his collar before tightening his tie.

- To prevent wrinkles between wears, roll up the tie, starting at the narrow end, and lay, seam-side down, in a drawer.

Shoulder Up

...

"The most important thing in a long-term relationship is that you have to be willing to compromise and to be unselfish. And you have to study your partner. Know what pushes somebody's buttons and then stay away from those things."
—Mildred Kalish

HOW TO BE A STRONG PARTNER

Step 1: Take responsibility for your own happiness. No one else, not even your honey, is capable of making you as happy as you're capable of making yourself. Expecting otherwise will only set you up for disappointment and your partner for failure.

Step 2: Be healthy. Exercise, eat well, and get your sleep, so you can be your best, most vibrant self. You'll be more capable of anything with a sharp mind and strong body.

Step 3: Talk—and listen. Have your own opinions and voice them, but also be open to hearing other points of view. Being an echo chamber or a bully serves no one.

Step 4: Make big decisions together, but minor ones alone. Self-sufficiency breeds confidence, and eliminating pesky trifles creates space for each of you to thrive.

Step 5: Champion your mate. You should be his or her first source of strength and comfort, aside from him- or herself. Be generous with praise and stingy with criticism.

Step 6: Spend quality time together, but not at the total expense of your own friendships and interests. If you never pursue anything but each other, your relationship will quickly lose its luster, as neither of you will have anything new or interesting to bring to it.

More Nifty Tips

- Fight fairly. When you disagree (and you will), do it respectfully. Nastiness will spoil any relationship, no matter how good the good times are.

- Dress to impress. Don't save your best for the rest of the world and always look a mess at home.

- Never, ever be too busy to give a smile, a hug, or a kiss.

Kindle Romance

· · ·

"My father always said for a happy marriage, don't think of yourself. Think of your partner and he should think of you and you will get along with each other and be happy."
—BEATRICE NEIDORF

HOW TO MAKE THE MOST OF A NIGHT IN

Step 1: Set aside one night every month (more frequently, if you can swing it), and make it known to your honey that it's "your night." Raise expectations by marking it on your calendar and talking up the evening.

Step 2: Eliminate distractions. Send the kids off to a friend or relative's house for the night. Turn off the television, shut down your computer, and silence the phones. Showing your honey that he or she is a priority and that there's nowhere else you'd rather be in the world is a big turn-on.

Step 3: Set the mood, according to your sweetie's taste. Punk rock and Pabst Blue Ribbon may put many more stars in his eyes than, say, Billie Holiday and bubbly. Don't get saddled by convention. Just find something that suits you both. Or, take turns. There's nothing wrong with beer one night and champagne the next.

Step 4: Activate your senses. That may mean enjoying a delicious meal, taking a bath, giving a backrub, or, wink, wink, slipping into something a little more comfortable. A short warning: Remember that the sole purpose of the evening is not to simply eat dinner. Take care not to overindulge, lest your stomach steal the spotlight from your sweetie.

Step 5: Surely, dear reader, you can figure this one out on your own. And if you can't, wait a few years and try again. It will come to you.

More Nifty Tips

- Trade planning duties. You take charge one night, and allow your honey to plan the next. If he's stumped, tell him what you like. That way, you'll both feel catered to and cared for.

- Be flexible. Expectations can bring pressure, so just be loose. Even if the evening doesn't go exactly as planned, it'll still be time together, which is valuable no matter what happens.

Welcome Your Honey Home

. . .

"Don't be afraid to say, 'I love you.' And make sure, if you're criticizing, it's really about something that makes a big difference. Don't sweat the little things."
—Grace Fortunato

How to Help Heal a Hard Day

Step 1: Be home when your sweetie returns from work, if you can help it. If you must step out, leave a kind note, stating where you've gone, when you expect to return, and how much you love him or her. For example, "Ran to the market. Be back in ten minutes. Love, me."

Step 2: Greet your mate at the door with a smile and kiss. Knowing that you make another person happy simply by showing up is enough to cheer anyone, even after the worst of days.

Step 3: Take his or her coat and bag and stow them away. It's not about waiting on your partner; it's just an easy way to give comfort. You are literally unburdening your honey.

Step 4: Listen and share. Sometimes all anyone needs is to feel heard and understood.

Step 5: Show your love. Small gestures, like a playful caress, a squeeze of the shoulder, or a hand on the knee, often mean more than large overtures, like a fancy dinner or a schmancy present.

There is a difference between knowing that someone cares for you and actually physically feeling it over and over again.

More Nifty Tips

- Share this page with your mate. Giving comfort to your partner is most definitely a two-way street.

- Don't allow your evening to devolve into a complain-a-thon. If you've both got a lot to unload, set a time (and time limit) to do it and then be done.

- When all else fails, pour a glass of wine and make out. Hey, don't knock it until you've tried it.

8

Saving

. . .

*With the future uncertain, you'll feel much
better with money in your pocket than,
say, a fancy new bag on your arm.*

Count Your Beans

. . .

*"It's about what you do with what you've got, not just what you've got.
Living your life to try to make more and more isn't a very good way to
live. You need to appreciate what you have and look to others who aren't
as lucky and feel that you're blessed and wonder why sometimes."*
—ALICE LOFT

HOW TO MAKE A BUDGET

Step 1: Track your spending. Keep a pencil and notepad with you
at all times. For three months, write down where every single penny
goes, whether it's for your rent or a pack of gum. That sounds like a
long time, but it's the only way to get an accurate read. Besides,
you'll get in the habit in no time.

Step 2: Examine your list. Divide your expenses into three major
categories: (1) fixed expenses, or recurring expenses like rent,
phone, utilities, etc.; (2) variable expenses, or essentials that vary in

price, like food, travel, and medical bills; and (3) optional expenses, like entertainment, clothes, and beauty buys. Then add up the totals in each, and multiply those tallies by four to find your projected yearly expenditures. Next, throw onto the list any annual layouts that may not be represented in your quarter-year sample, including any insurance payments, memberships, seasonal splurges (lift tickets, Christmas presents, annual vacation, subscriptions). Calculate your grand total. Yell ai-ooooga! And then put your eyeballs back in your head.

Step 3: Figure out your annual income. Add to your salary any sources of dough you can definitely count on, including bonus pay or dividends. Now compare your income to your cash outlay from step 2. Are you earning more than you're spending? If so, wahoo! Are you spending more than you're earning? Uh-oh, that's trouble.

Step 4: Grow your money. Even if you're in the black, there are probably places where you can find extra savings. (Don't think of it as skimping. Think of it as paying yourself first, because that's exactly what you're doing.) Start by examining your optional expenses, and see where you can find more cash. Do you really need new shoes, or can you just shine up your old ones? (See page 115 for instructions.) Must you buy a $9 sandwich every day at work, or can you pack a lunch? (For ideas, see page 185). Do you need to take those yoga classes at that fancy studio for $14 a pop or could you pick up a DVD and do them at home sometimes? Once you identify where you can save, readjust your monthly allowances and stick to them.

Step 5: Know your goals. It's easier to live within your budget if you know what you're saving for. Jot down the financial goals you'd like to achieve in the next year and in the next five years. Whenever you feel the urge to splurge, read your goals once more to help you stay focused.

More Nifty Tips

- Try to put at least 10 percent of your pretax income into your just-for-emergencies savings account and another 10 percent into a retirement fund.

- Start with small, realistic cuts and, if you can swing more, make them. That way, you'll never be caught sitting in the dark wondering, "How did I convince myself that electricity was a luxury?"

- Until you have three to six months of savings stashed, refrain from major splurging. Once you have your nest egg, you can afford the occasional indulgence, guilt-free, because you've saved for it.

Banish Debt

. . .

"My money advice: Don't spend it. Hold on to as much as you can!"
—RUTH ROWEN

HOW TO SHOP WITHOUT CREDIT

Step 1: Leave your plastic at home. If you slip your credit card in a desk drawer, rather than your wallet, you'll be far less likely to splurge on impulse buys. Keeping it in a safe place will protect you should temptation strike.

Step 2: Stash your cash. Hit your ATM once a week, withdraw your allotted allowance, and don't tap it again until the following week. You'll consider your purchases much more carefully when you literally have to part with the money in your hand, and you'll be more mindful of your budget when you actually see your dollars dwindle. If you burn through your allowance for the week, that's it, stop spending.

Step 3: Plan ahead. Evaluate and adjust your budget in order to save for bigger purchases. Even after you've found a way to stockpile the necessary dough, carefully consider if you need the item. Write down your dream purchase, along with its price, and the pros and cons of making the buy. Are those shoes worth giving up your weekly bowling night with the girls? Which will make you happier in the long run? Do you really need a new cell phone, or does your old one work just fine? If, upon closer inspection, you can afford what you want and you need it, buy it in cash and enjoy it, stress-free!

More Nifty Tips

- Prioritize your life. Remember, you won't find lasting happiness in any store. If you feel empty, stop buying crap you don't need, and make friends (see page 233), volunteer (see page 240) or find love (see page 194). All are much more valuable than anything you can charge.

- For bigger-ticket items, say $30 or more, install a waiting period. That way, you'll think more carefully about what you buy.

- Just say no to plastic. Keep one or two low-interest, zero-fee cards, and pay them off monthly, so you can establish good credit, which is helpful when you'd like to get a home or car loan. Every other promotional offer that lands in your mailbox? Cut it up.

Find Balance

· · ·

"Learn to enjoy what you have and stop wanting so much. Life is about loving each other. Get what you can, enjoy what you have, aspire to higher things, but not to a point where it becomes an obsession. Be happy with what you have and continue to strive for more."
—GRACE FORTUNATO

HOW TO RECONCILE YOUR CHECKBOOK

Step 1: Save all your receipts for every single financial transaction you make, including deposits, ATM withdrawals, and purchases via debit, cash, or check. File them weekly in a designated folder or drawer.

Step 2: Double-check your records. Once a month, after you receive your bank statement, sort through your receipts and canceled checks and account for every transaction on your statement. Place a check mark along each verified purchase or deposit. Then add up your receipts and your bank transactions to make sure both tallies match.

Step 3: Account for stragglers. If you've written checks or made purchases or deposits that haven't yet appeared on your bank statement, adjust your balance accordingly, so you'll know how much money you really have in the bank.

Step 4: Separate your receipts. Place business expenses in one folder and personal expenses in another, so come tax season, you'll have an easier time sorting your paperwork.

More Nifty Tips

- If you see charges on your statement that you don't recall, especially if they're at, say, HotBunzs.fr or some other website or overseas shop, first double-check your memory. What *did* you do after that fourth glass of pinot grigio last Friday? Went straight to bed? Ring your bank immediately to alert their fraud department.

- Pay your monthly bills right after you reconcile your balances. That way, you'll know exactly how much money you have and you'll be less likely to bounce a check (and incur those nasty fees).

- Try to keep your bank balance above the minimum to avoid monthly checking fees. You could save a bundle.

Chill Out

• • •

"We didn't have no air conditioners or fans or nothing. If the wind was blowing we was cool. If it wasn't, we weren't."
—Elouise Bruce

How to Save on Energy Costs

Warm Up During the Winter

Step 1: Bundle up. You don't have to wear a Snuggie twenty-four hours a day, but do dress warmly (and in layers), even inside. Put on a wool sweater, warm pants, silk long johns if you've got them, and some toasty socks. If, in December, you're wearing a T-shirt and shorts inside (and you don't live in the South), then you're paying way too much for your heating bill.

Step 2: Pipe down. Set your thermostat to as low a setting as is comfy when you're home, and to 58 degrees when you're away or sleeping. For every degree you crank it down in the day, you'll save about 2 percent of your bill. Adding an extra blanket to your bed and sleeping in cooler temps can save you up to 7 percent.

Step 3: Use solar power. You don't need any fancy panels to harness the power of the sun. Just throw open your curtains on sunny days and let the rays warm your home.

Step 4: Hunker down. If you're lucky enough to have an extra room (or two or five) that you don't use, close their doors to trap the warmth where you live. Why pay to heat the entire house, when you hang out only in three rooms?

Step 5: Break wind. If you feel a draft by a door or window, you've likely got some leaks. Seal the frames with caulk. And lay draft stoppers, usually cloth tubes filled with sand or beans, across the thresholds of your doors.

Step 6: Use your senses. During the chilly season, decorate with reds, golds, and oranges to trick your mind into feeling warm. Add lots of texture, too, by piling up chunky blankets and soft pillows, to make a perfect cuddling spot for you and your honey (and your dogs, if you've got them).

Step 7: Bake yourself a pie. (See page 19 for tips.) If the heat of the oven doesn't warm you, the promise of pie should help.

Cool Down During the Summer

Step 1: Embrace the heat. Unless you live in the Lut Desert in Iran, which once reached 157 degrees (the hottest land temperature ever recorded), try to refrain from running your air conditioner twenty-four hours a day. If you're wearing a sweater inside in July (and you live in the Northern Hemisphere), you're paying too much for your cooling bill.

Step 2: Be smart. Pull your shades down to block the sun, open your windows when the breeze is cool, and avoid using any heat-generating appliances (your oven, dishwasher, and dryer) until after the sun sets.

Step 3: Plant a tree. The branches will not only provide natural shade for your house, but also for your yard. Hang a hammock, enjoy the breeze, and have a lemonade.

More Nifty Tips

- If you've got big gaps around your doors and windows, add insulation before caulking. You can even use scraps from your rag bag, like wool, corduroy, or any heavy material.

- To make your own draft stopper, measure the width of your door and add 10 inches. Cut a piece of material that length by 12 inches wide. Sew the long sides together, fill it with rice, beans, or sand, and tie off the ends with a ribbon.

- Install a cheaper-than-A/C ceiling fan to create a cool breeze in the summer. In the reverse direction, it'll circulate warm air in the winter, too.

- Swap out your lightbulbs for Energy Star–approved bulbs. Each bulb will save you thirty dollars over the course of its lifetime.

- If you're worried about being too hot, just remember: Animals sweat, men perspire, ladies glow. Let yourself glow, girl.

Conquer Cravings

· · ·

"We didn't have money to throw around at all, so we always had to think about things before we bought them. It was a decision with pros and cons. We were brought up with a sense of being careful."
—ALICE LOFT

HOW TO GROCERY SHOP

Step 1: Have a snack. If you hit the grocery story on an empty stomach, there is a grave danger that by aisle 4, you'll be hungry enough to think that those glow-in-the-dark Hostess Sno Balls (yes, they actually exist) look like something you'd want to swallow. Save yourself! Eat an apple first.

Step 2: Make a list and stick to it. Impulse buys rarely include good-for-you foods. Honestly, which would you be more likely to toss into your cart on a whim: a bag of potato chips or a bag of potatoes? Right, thought so. Which is more expensive? Yep, doubly thought so.

Step 3: Shop the perimeter. Think of the grocery store the same way you'd think of a male model. Everything you should be putting in your mouth is on the outside, and there's hardly anything of substance on the inside. You'll generally find veggies on one end, meat in the back, and dairy on the other end. Everything in between is more skippable (and expensive).

Step 4: Buy seasonally. The farther fruits and veggies have to travel to get to you, the more expensive (and less tasty) they'll be. Opt for locally grown produce, which will be nicer on your wallet and your taste buds.

More Nifty Tips

- Markups on prepared-for-you foods are sky-high, so to save money, buy a block of cheese instead of the shredded stuff; a whole chicken, instead of boneless breasts; a bunch of spinach, rather than prewashed leaves.

- Opt for store brands over name brands; they generally have the same nutritional content.

Drive a Bargain

. . .

"Every day, the carts would come by selling veggies or fruit. We bargained down the price by saying, 'It's too much' or 'I can't pay that much.' You had to be insistent, but you eventually got the price you wanted. Sometimes they'd stick to their guns and wouldn't budge, but if you started to walk away, then you got the price."
—Grace Fortunato

How to Negotiate a Better Price

Step 1: Work up your courage. You'll never get a discount if you don't ask for one. Almost everything is on sale, if you know how to haggle.

Step 2: Know the market. Be realistic about the price you want. If every merchant is selling a bag of apples for $2.50 to $3.50 a pop, don't expect to buy one for a quarter. But do ask your seller to match the lowest price. If you're buying more than one, ask for a bigger break.

Step 3: Know your audience. You'll be more likely to get discounts at locally owned stores rather than multinational chains and from managers rather than clerks. If you're dealing with someone who can't offer you a discount, kindly ask to speak with his superior. Be charming, if you can. Nobody wants to go the extra mile for a poo head.

Step 4: Look for flaws. This may feel a bit shady but it really isn't. Examine the item you'd like to buy for any imperfections. If it's got any stains, scratches, pulls, or dents, you'll be more likely to get an automatic damaged-good discount, which is usually at least 10 percent off.

Step 5: Offer to pay in cash. Stores have to pay a small fee to credit card companies if you use plastic. By paying in cash, they'll likely pass that savings on to you, if you ask for it.

Step 6: Walk away. Sometimes the threat of losing the sale is enough to make the seller cave. If he doesn't, just keeping on walking. You've already determined that the price is not right.

More Nifty Tips

- Be firm. Serious hagglers actually get better deals than sweet ones. When you get down to the nitty-gritty deal-making, try not to giggle.

- Be friendly. Insulting the seller or his products won't make him want to do you any favors.

Spot a Deal

• • •

*"If you want something you can't afford, save for it
until you can pay for it."*
—Sue Westheimer Ransohoff

How to Clip Coupons

Step 1: Make your list. Whether you're hitting the grocery store or the hardware store, decide what you need to buy first and write it down. Seeing your shopping goals on paper will help prevent you from being seduced by discounts. Remember, if you buy something you don't need, it's not a good deal for you, no matter how little it costs.

Step 2: Hunt for discounts. Scan your local paper, especially the Sunday edition, or search the Internet for coupons on the products you need. No luck? Go to the manufacturer's or store's website. Oftentimes, they'll offer coupons that you can print out and bring with you to the store.

Step 3: Check for bonus deals. Some stores offer double coupon days, which means you can save, say, $2 with your $1 off coupon on certain days. Other stores will honor coupons issued by competitors or even expired coupons. Call to get the scoop.

Step 4: Cash them in. Bring your coupons with you when you shop, and present them before the cashier rings you up. After you pay, check your receipt and celebrate your savings by dancing out of the store. (Suggestion: Try moonwalking. It's cool. Just make sure there's no one behind you.)

More Nifty Tips

- Never buy something online without using a promo code. Take two precious seconds to enter the retailer's name and "coupon code" into Google, and you'll usually be able to score free shipping at the very least. That's time well spent.

- Keep a stash. If you spot great coupons that you might be able to use in the future, clip them and tuck them into an envelope, so you can redeem them when you're ready.

Make Change

* * *

"Pay as you go along. Don't have a lot of debt. And realize what your money is worth."
—Jean Dinsmore

How to Throw a Yard Sale

Step 1: Gather your merchandise. In this case, getting organized can also mean getting rich (well, sort of), so go through your closets, search under the bed, and tidy up your garage. If you find anything that you (1) no longer use, (2) never did use, or (3) don't even recognize, put it in the sale. Gather all your unused treasures in a designated, out-of-the-way spot, and once you accumulate enough, set a date for your sale.

Step 2: Get the word out. Advertise your sale by telling your friends and family, placing an ad in your local newspaper or online, and hanging a few flyers around your neighborhood. Make sure to include all details: the date of your sale (and rain date, if you set one), the start and finish times, your address, and some highlights of what you'll be selling. You would not believe how many people would like your mint-condition poster of Rick Springfield.

Step 3: Tag your wares. Write your asking price on a piece of masking tape affixed to each item or, if you want to get fancy, on a piece of cardboard tied on with ribbon. Keep your prices simple (go for $5, rather than $5.49), so you don't have to make crazy change all day. And make your tags visible. Some customers may be too shy to ask for the price, so if they don't see a tag, you'll lose the sale.

Step 4: Prepare your "store." The day before the sale, go to the bank and get $50 worth of change in fives, ones, and quarters, and tuck it into an old toolbox or another secure box. And tidy up your yard. You want to draw in potential customers, not drive them away.

Step 5: Be a master merchandiser. The night before the sale, arrange your sale items by type (clothing, electronics, knickknacks, etc.) or by price ($1, $5, $10, etc.) on tables or blankets, which you can carry outside first thing in the morning. If you have fancy clothes, string them up on a clothesline to make them look stylish.

Step 6: Open for business! At the designated hour, move your merch outside. Deal hounds tend to show up early, so be ready right away. Smile and chat with the people who show. Not only is it good manners, but it'll help you sell more stuff and, even more important, have more fun!

More Nifty Tips

- If you have unsold wares, don't throw them away! Take them to Goodwill or donate them to the charity of your choice.

- Team up with the folks next door and plan a sale together. It's a neighborly thing to do—and you'll get twice the foot traffic.

- Run a heavy-duty extension cord outside, so you can plug in any electronic goods to demonstrate that they are in fine working shape. Also, have a mirror handy for anyone considering a clothes or sunglasses purchase.

- Remember, your goal is to clear the clutter, not to become Donald Trump, so don't try to drive too hard of a bargain.

Save for Later

. . .

HOW TO START A RAINY DAY FUND

Step 1: Open a new savings account. You should aim to have three to six months' worth of savings socked away in case of emergency. Choose an account that carries FDIC insurance, no minimum fees, and, if you can, at least a 4 percent interest rate.

Step 2: Divert funds. Whenever you receive a paycheck, ask your bank to automatically transfer 10 percent to your new account. Chances are, if you never see it, you'll hardly even miss it. And if you do, well, then learn to make do. Tiny budgetary adjustments, like making your own coffee at home or driving a little less, make a big difference.

Step 3: Revel in your success. Check in on your savings a few times a year to ensure adequate growth.

More Nifty Tips

- If you're planning for a new baby, house, or career, open a separate savings account for the venture and give it a name that means something to you. For example, "Money for diapers,"

"My big chance at my dream job," or "No more couch surfing." That'll help you tap into it for its designated purpose only.

- Charge yourself interest. Vow never to dip into your SOS shoe box before you deposit the funds, but if you must, require yourself to pay it back, plus 10 percent.

- Hey you, wake up! This money stuff is utterly boring and very unglamorous, but very important. Step to it!

- Get lucky! For small savings, choose your favorite denomination, whether it's nickels, dimes, quarters, singles, or fives. Whenever you receive any of your lucky money as change, sock it away in a jar or shoe box. Deposit contents monthly into your savings account.

Live a Richer Life
· · ·

*"We lived in a rural area, close to a railroad track, and people
who had no jobs would ride the rods on the freight trains. They'd wander
into the area and ask if we had anything for them to eat because they
were hungry and had no means of support. My mother always fixed a
plate and they sat on the porch and ate it. It was the normal thing to do.
It didn't seem special."*
—ALICE LOFT

HOW TO SHARE YOUR GOOD FORTUNE
(EVEN WHEN TIMES ARE TIGHT)

Step 1: Check your heart. Who you give to is much more important than how much you give. Identify your goals, and then rank
them from the most important to the least. Find a charity (local or
global, small or large) that supports your desires. The better match
you find, the better you'll feel about your gift, and the more likely
you'll be to keep on giving. Oh, happiness! Such a vicious cycle.

Step 2: Check your budget. If you can spare some change at the
end of each month, please do. Collect quarters in a coin jar. Or,
round each paycheck to the nearest zero and earmark the rest for
charity. (If you earn $213, designate $3 for donations.)

Step 3: Write that check. Sometime this is the hardest part, but
it's also the most rewarding. Promise. Can't get the pen to paper?
Schedule automatic monthly payments with your bank to your char-

ity of choice, so you don't even have to think about it. Even if it's just a few bucks, it can add up.

Step 4: Plan for spontaneity. When times are tough, you may encounter people in need every day. Keep an extra piece or two of fruit with you to distribute when called upon. Surely, it will be much appreciated.

More Nifty Tips

- Ask your company if it has a matching program. Oftentimes, whatever you give, it'll double.

- Donate your time if you can't afford to donate your money. Many organizations rely on the skills and kindness of strangers to stay afloat.

- When you see a great sale at the grocery store, say, five cans of tuna for $5 dollars, stock up and split your bounty with your local food bank.

- Clear your clutter seasonally, and deliver your out-of-use goods to your local thrift store. It's a twofer: You'll get organized and feel satisfied.

Shop for Free

...

"When I was real little and our neighbors wanted vegetables, we traded with them. They'd come around and say they'd want some, and I'd just go, 'Yeah,' and I'd go with them to the garden. It was just a new person over and something to do."
—ELOUISE BRUCE

HOW TO BARTER

Step 1: Divide a piece of paper into two columns. In the first, list objects you might like to trade (e.g., *Battlestar Galactica* season 3 DVDs, a set of naughty salt-'n'-pepper shakers, an old Mac) and skills you have to offer (e.g., pie making, button sewing, scarf knitting). In the second, list goods or services you need or want (e.g., *Battlestar Galactica* season 4 DVDs, a piano lesson, a box of handmade thank-you cards).

Step 2: Open your pie hole. Ask your friends or acquaintances if they'd be willing to barter with you. If you have good relationships with any local business owners, whether it's your lawyer, accountant, or that cool jewelry designer down the street, broach the subject of trading services with them, too (of course, *before* you do business). If you're rejected, don't take it personally.

Step 3: If you are friends only with ultracapitalist banker types who respond only to green, first, reevaluate your life. Next, go online to find other traders. Two good starting points: FreeCycle.org and CraigsList.org. Both sites allow you to post your goods and services and search the marketplace to see what others are offering.

Step 4: Keep spreading the word. As the word about your openness to trade gets out, people will begin to come to you.

More Nifty Tips

- If you know someone with a garden, orchard, or farm, offer to pulls weeds, prune trees, or pick vegetables in return for a small harvest of your own (say, a basket of tomatoes, a peck of apples, or a pan of beans).

- If you're thinking this all sounds too terribly awkward, well, it can be at first. But the reward both parties will feel after making a good trade makes it all worth it.

9

Joining

. . .

Your community is your safety net. Don't be a loner.
The more you give, the more you get.

Be Neighborly

• • •

"If a person moved into the neighborhood, you always took a pot of coffee over and a cake made from scratch. You got to know people and you took care of each other. Not that you did big things, but I always felt that in a pinch I could always call on my neighbor."
— NIKKI SPANOF CHRISANTHON

HOW TO ENJOY THE FOLKS NEXT DOOR

Step 1: Start off right. Welcome new folks to the neighborhood with some baked goods, a bouquet of flowers, a bottle of wine, or just a smile and a chat. (If you're the newbie and your neighbors are shy, introduce yourself.) The better neighbor you are, the better neighbor you'll have.

Step 2: Lend a hand. If you see your neighbor struggling with a grocery bag, offer help. If they're heading out of town, offer to keep an eye on their house, collect their mail, feed their dog, or water their plants. If they need to borrow something, like a cup of sugar or a jigsaw, be generous. You'll find that when you need help, they'll be there for you, too.

Step 3: Set boundaries. Resist the temptation to snoop, lurk, or peep over the hedges. Aim for friendly, not smothering. Respect your neighbors' privacy, and they'll respect yours, too.

Step 4: Pipe down. There is at most a yard and at least a thin wall that separates you from the folks next door, so keep your noise to a minimum. Calm your yipping dog, turn down your hip-hop, run your vacuum cleaner during the day, and try not to get too, ahem, carried away at night. If in doubt, remember the Golden Rule, and ask yourself what you'd like to hear your neighbors doing.

Step 5: Keep it clean. If the Maysles show up at your door asking permission to shoot *Grey Gardens 2*, you'll know you've let a few things slide. Keep your lawn reasonably manicured, and your yard and house free of trash and clutter. You want your neighbors to enjoy living next to you, not cringe whenever they pass by.

More Nifty Tips

- If your kids befriend the neighbors' kids, hooray! Just call them home for meals, lest they become a burden to the folks next door.

- Don't judge. Even if your neighbors aren't exactly like you— say, they're a couple of very handsome men, a family who reen- acts the nativity each December in their front yard, or a couple who spends their Sundays in renaissance fair outfits—open your heart. You can learn the most from people who are the most different from you. Heck, you may even learn to love them.

Keep the Peace

• • •

"We didn't have any problems in our neighborhood. Each person, whether it was the butcher, shoemaker, or barber, would sweep the sidewalk and put any trash at the curb."
—Grace Fortunato

How to Deal with a Problem
in Your Neighborhood

Step 1: Assess the situation. When you live in close quarters, chances are your neighbors will annoy you at some point, just as you'll annoy them. If they've committed a onetime offense—say, their dog pooped in your yard, their trash blew into your driveway, or they played "The Electric Slide" embarrassingly loud one night—give them a break. But if it happens with regularity, or if they're doing something that can harm your happiness or property value, proceed to step 2.

Step 2: Nip it in the bud. If you're friendly with your neighbor, give her a ring, or better yet, invite her over for coffee some afternoon. Without anger, judgment, or accusation, discuss your problem openly and honestly. You just might find that she had no idea she was bothering you and would be more than happy to change her ways. Or, she may just need a little help, so offer to chip in.

Step 3: If that doesn't work, or you feel at all threatened, enlist help. Report the issue to the local authorities (anonymously, if you'd like) and ask your other neighbors, including any merchants, to do the same.

Step 4: Organize your neighborhood. Consider calling a meeting with your neighbors to discuss possible solutions to whatever problem is afflicting you. You'll have a better shot at combating the nuisance (or danger) if you join together.

More Nifty Tips

- If you get to know your neighbors in the first place (see page 222), you'll be better equipped to deal with any problems that may arise in the future.

- Never confront your neighbors in anger. If you're too steamed up, have a martini (see page 259), go to sleep (see page 171), wake up happy (see page 3), and then approach them the next day after you've chilled out. You never want to say or do something you might regret. After all, you have to live next to these people.

Expand Your Circle

· · ·

"You have to be a friend to have a friend."
—BEATRICE NEIDORF

HOW TO MAKE FRIENDS

Step 1: Leave your living room. Chances are, new friends are not going to spring up between your sofa and the television. To find buds, you have to step out.

Step 2: Be a joiner. If you're a jock, sign up for a team; a reader, join a book club; a lush, take a wine-tasting class. Whatever your pleasure, put yourself in situations where you'll meet people who share at least one common interest. It'll give you something to gab about, and the rest will come more easily.

Step 3: Kindle womance. Take a chance, and ask one (or more) of your new acquaintances on a girlfriend date, say, for a beer after your stitch 'n' bitch circle, or to the latest Catherine Opie exhibit between your photography classes. Your invitation will likely be well received, and your risk will bring rewards.

Step 4: Be a keeper. If you want to keep your circle growing, be a good friend: Listen, celebrate your pals' successes, support them through their failures, and seek out fun together.

More Nifty Tips

• Diversify your friendships. It's okay to have a work bud, a party pal, a gym mate, a hometown friend, and others. Everyone doesn't have to be a soul mate, and placing unfair expectations on each will only lead to disappointment.

• Value quality over quantity. It's not the number of contacts you have in your iPhone that counts. It's the number of friends who will answer your call when you need them.

• Even if you have hundreds of friends on Facebook, that doesn't mean you shouldn't have in-the-flesh friends, too. There is no virtual substitute for a hug or a belly laugh.

• Be patient. It can take years to establish intimacy. Instead of worrying about what you don't get from your friends, feel blessed for what they give you.

Summon Support

. . .

"I've had difficulties in my life, and the people I'm close to know when I'm struggling. If it's a friend or neighbor, they'll say, 'If you need me, I'm here.' When you get the courage, you can say, 'I need someone to talk to. Can you listen to me?' And if I know someone is having a problem, I'll say, 'I'm here if you need me. Just call.'"
—GRACE FORTUNATO

HOW TO ASK FOR HELP

Step 1: Speak up. If you're feeling overwhelmed, don't suffer in silence. Instead, hold your head high, take a deep breath, and reach out to someone you trust. Opening up to a friend will make you feel supported and her feel valued. It's a win-win situation.

Step 2: Be specific about your needs. Do you require sympathy, guidance, or action? You'll be more likely to get what you need if you ask for it directly.

Step 3: Say thanks. Let your pal know you'll return the favor anytime.

Step 4: Feel proud. By seeking help, you've not only come closer to solving your problem, but you've also demonstrated tremendous resourcefulness and bravery. Pound your chest a few times, or pump your fist in the air. You rock!

More Nifty Tips

- If you're really struggling, try helping someone else. Not only will you feel instantly empowered, but you'll also gain confidence in your own problem-solving abilities.

- Don't look for a quick fix (or all the answers) from your confidant. Know that the most they can do is guide you toward change—you'll have to do the rest yourself.

Cultivate Culture

. . .

"Don't forget, there's a big world out there that can use your talents."
—Lucile Frisbee

How to Start a Book Club

Step 1: Check out the scene. Before you start your own book club, make sure there isn't one around already that you might like to join. If you can't find one (or you found one you didn't totally dig), proceed to step 2.

Step 2: Assess your agenda. Is the purpose of your book club to foster cultural criticism or to have an excuse to see friends and drink martinis? Would you like to analyze every Danielle Steele book ever written or get through the classics? The clearer you are about your intentions up front, the more successful your club will be.

Step 3: Recruit new members. Depending on the answer you came up with in step 2, invite readers from your social circle, workplace, and community. If you don't get enough members through word of mouth, try making fliers or placing an ad online. Ideally, you'll have between three and twelve book buddies.

Step 4: Schedule your first meeting. If your group includes close friends, feel free to have it at your home. If it includes strangers, meet at a café, bar, or library so everyone feels comfy.

Step 5: Set the rules. During your first meeting, get to know one another and then decide (1) how you'll choose the books you'll read; (2) where, when, and how often you'll meet; (3) who will lead the discussion; and most important; (4) what, if any, snacks and cocktails will be served. Once you've got that business settled, choose your first page-turner and get busy reading.

More Nifty Tips

- Food and drink (especially drink) are not necessary for a good book discussion, but they often help to make it feel less like homework and more like a hoot.

- Don't be afraid to speak up, even if you're new to the group. You'll learn more and have more fun if you actively participate.

- Be respectful. If the host chooses a book you're not crazy about, read it anyway. You may be surprised by how many genres you can enjoy.

- Everything about the book is up for discussion. Even if you hated it or couldn't get past the first fifteen pages, remember that you've got something to contribute—your opinion.

- If you're nervous about hosting, look online for reading group guides. Most publishers will prepare and post them before their books hit the shelves.

Lend a Hand

• • •

"I get as much out of volunteering as I give."
—BEATRICE NEIDORF

HOW TO VOLUNTEER

Step 1: Match your skills with your passions. There is an infinite number of ways to make the world a better place, and it's up to you to determine how you can best help. Ask yourself what you have to offer and what goals you'd like to achieve. The more meaningful (and satisfying) the work is to you, the more likely you'll be to stick with it and make real change.

Step 2: Make time—and be realistic about it. You don't need an extra twenty hours a week to be a worthy volunteer. Many organizations can use whatever help they can get, even if it's for just one day. If you're tight on time, sign up for a park cleanup, hand out water at a charity 5K, or offer to make something for a school bake sale. If you can swing a more regular gig of, say, an hour or two a week (and you certainly can if you've ever found yourself watching reality show reruns), visit Serve.gov to find opportunities near you.

Step 3: Honor your commitmen: Show up on time, call in if you can't make it, and be respectful of all the people with whom you're working.

Step 4: Stick with it. It takes time to make volunteering a habit and to see the fruits of your labor. Allow yourself a few weeks or months to find your groove. Soon enough, you'll see the difference you've made, and you'll feel good knowing that you've helped make the world a better place. This is your cue to start singing "We Are the World."

More Nifty Tips

- If you're not totally digging your volunteer work, don't stop volunteering altogether. Gracefully bow out and find a better fit elsewhere.

- Try a volunteer vacation! What would you rather write on your postcards home: "Dear Mom, I won the wet T-shirt contest last night and slept in until noon today" or "Dear Mom, I rescued twelve baby sea turtles today!" Find some cool opportunities at GlobalVolunteers.org.

Say It with a Smile

. . .

"Never hurt anybody intentionally. Always think before you open your mouth, treat everybody the way you'd want them to treat you, and always respect their feelings."
—Nikki Spanof Chrisanthon

How to Win an Utterly Silly Argument (Without Saying Much at All)

Step 1: Listen. Every person has her own truth, ahem, even if it's wrong. Hearing somebody out doesn't mean you must agree with her.

Step 2: Reflect your pal's emotions. Rather than engaging in a heated point-by-point discussion, offer a gentle assessment of her stance and/or state of mind (e.g., "You seem to feel really passionately about this").

Step 3: Introduce common ground. Asking affirmative questions, or questions to which she'll answer yes, may help her remember that you're a friend, not a foe.

Step 4: Resolve it. Once you identify any ideas you have in common, celebrate those. Remember, you don't have to fully agree with someone to appreciate her feelings or experiences.

More Nifty Tips

- Stay calm and smile. What you do is often as important as what you say.

- Keep an open mind. Realize that most arguments are just plain silly and that there is a teensy tiny chance that you just might be wrong.

- If all else fails, say something nice—anything you can think of, doesn't matter—and just walk away.

Get Heard

• • •

*"I'm enormously involved in the political process. Over the years, you
get to know all the people. I care about all of my causes, but I get a benefit
from being involved as well. I'm not that wonderful. I'm just
having a ball!"*
—Sue Westheimer Ransohoff

How to Speak Your Mind
at a Town Hall Meeting

Step 1: Rehearse your speech. Jot down a few notes about what
you'd like to say, and run through your bit in front of friends and
family. Practicing it in front of a few people will help you feel more
confident when you deliver it in front of a larger group.

Step 2: Say your piece. When it's your turn to speak, introduce
yourself, and no matter how high your passions are running, make
your well-reasoned points calmly, clearly, quickly, and carefully. If
you speak with conviction, others will listen. If you shout, they'll
tune you out. (If you rhyme, you'll have a good time!)

Step 3: Thank your audience for listening, and then sit down and
listen, too. You might be surprised by what you can learn.

More Nifty Tips

- If you practice your speech at home, rehearse it in different locations throughout your house. That way, you won't be thrown by the new setting.

- When you do approach the microphone, don't tap it and say, "Is this thing on?" Just start talking, and you'll know.

- Dress professionally. People will bestow your words with more weight if you look like an upstanding member of the community, rather than an interloper who just showed up for the free cookies and juice.

Write for Your Rights

● ● ●

"Good citizenship requires that you get involved."
—LUCILE FRISBEE

HOW TO WRITE A LETTER TO YOUR REPRESENTATIVE

Step 1: Identify your delegates. Your own reps will be more responsive to your concerns, since it is their duty to act in your best interest. Plus, hello, they also rely on your vote to get elected. You can find their names and addresses online or in the blue pages of your phone book. If you've got access to neither, call your local librarian.

Step 2: State your purpose. Start by formally addressing your recipient and then state clearly and immediately the purpose of your correspondence (e.g., "Dear Senator, Please listen to your grandmother. You could learn a thing or two from her.")

Step 3: Identify yourself. In one or two sentences, explain why you have authority on this position (e.g., "I've been listening to her my whole life and can vouch that she has something valuable to teach").

Step 4: Make your case. Bolster your position by citing facts rather than emotion (e.g., "Your grandmother, having survived the Great Depression, has proven herself to be much smarter and more resourceful than you. She would've never advised you to lead us into such debt or to fracture our communities. Plus, she knows how to make a mean pie *and* sing in harmony.")

Step 5: Reiterate your request and offer advance gratitude just in case a little courtesy (or guilt) will get you anywhere (e.g., "So, please call Grammy and listen to her. Thanks so much!").

Step 6: Sign your name and date it. Don't forget to include your contact information should your rep like to reply (e.g., "Love, Mom").

More Nifty Tips

- Consider submitting your letter to your local paper.

- Ask your friends, family, and neighbors to write letters as well if they share your views and passion.

- Go ultramodern. E-mailing your reps works just as well, if you want to get all cutting-edge.

Entertaining

...

Make your own fun.
You'll be happier,
and richer (in all ways), for it.

Get Better with Age

. . .

"We made our own wine. Some of it turned out, some of it didn't. Of course, we got drunk, too. One time, we let it ferment in our family room, and we all got dizzy from the fumes!"
—Nikki Spanof Chrisanthon

How to Make Dandelion Wine

Step 1: Kick off your shoes, go outside on a sunny afternoon, and pick 2 quarts' worth of fresh dandelion blossoms. You need only the flower petals, so pluck them from their heads, and give them a good wash. (The leaves and stems will bitter your wine.)

Step 2: Place your harvest in a large pot, and pour 1 gallon of boiling water over the top. Let steep for 3 days, and then strain the tea through a cheesecloth into a second pot, squeezing all the juice out of the blooms. Compost your flowers (see page 43).

Step 3: Stir in 9 cups (or 4 pounds) granulated sugar and the juice of 4 oranges and 3 lemons.

Step 4: In ½ cup lukewarm water, dissolve 1 packet champagne yeast (available at winemaking supply stores) or active dry yeast (available at any grocery store), and stir it into your pot.

Step 5: Once it's mixed, pour the wine into a 2- to 3-gallon jug (or several 1-gallon jugs). To prevent it from turning to vinegar, stretch a large balloon over the mouth of the jug. (The balloon will inflate as the wine ferments.) Or, even better, plug it with an air lock, available for a couple of bucks at any winemaking supply store. Set it in a dark closet for about 6 weeks.

Step 6: Strain through a cheesecloth to remove sediment. Repeat as necessary, until the wine runs clear. Pour into bottles or jars. Cork or screw lids on tightly. Serve chilled. It's like drinking pure sunshine.

More Nifty Tips

- For the best flavor, pick your dandelions when the blossoms are in full bloom.

- Store the blossoms in the freezer if you can't make the wine immediately.

- Try spicing things up by adding orange and lemon zest, cloves, ginger, cherries, whatever you desire.

- For even smoother wine, add 1 pound of raisins during step 3.

Quench Your Thirst

. . .

"We started out having a drink with company, and then having a drink now and then for no reason. We were never known for imbibing overly, but when we did, we were sorry the next day."

—ALICE LOFT

HOW TO BREW YOUR OWN BEER

Step 1: Gather your equipment. You can round up all of it on your own or visit a home brew supply store (online or in person) and pick up a starter kit for about $65. Totally worth it! Here's what you need:

- One 3- to 4-gallon stockpot
- One long metal spoon
- One 6- to 6½-gallon glass carboy (one of those giant bottles that spring water typically comes in) with a cap
- One 5-gallon (or larger) plastic bucket
- 6 feet of clear plastic tubing (about ⅜ inch in diameter)
- One air lock
- One rubber stopper with a hole in the middle (like a doughnut)
- One funnel
- One thermometer
- Some bleach
- One empty milk or wine jug
- A shot of vodka (two, if you want one)
- 60 12-ounce beer bottles

- 60 new bottle caps
- One bottle capper

Step 2: Gather your ingredients. Only four things go into most beers: water, malt, hops, and yeast. (You'll also need some corn sugar for bottling.) For a basic bitter, pick up 5 pounds light or amber malt extract, 2 ounces Cascade pellet hops, a package of ale yeast, and, while you're at it, some corn sugar.

Step 3: Wash your fermentation equipment, and then do your best to sanitize it, or your beer will spoil. Here's how: Fill your carboy with water, add 5 tablespoons bleach, and give a good swishing. Then fill a pot (or sink) with another gallon of water, add 1 tablespoon bleach, and drop in your thermometer, funnel, carboy cap, rubber tubing, rubber stopper, and a pair of rubber gloves. Let everything sit for 20 minutes, then rinse it all with hot (or even boiling) water. From now on, touch these items only while wearing your sanitized rubber gloves.

Step 4: Now, the fun part: Brew your beer! Heat 1½ gallons water in your pot, and once it's steaming hot, add your malt extract and 1 ounce hops, stirring constantly until it dissolves. Then bring your kettle to a full rolling boil. (Keep an eye on it, or it will bubble over.) After 40 minutes, add ½ ounce hops to round out the flavor. Boil for another 17 minutes. Add the remaining ½ ounce hops for aroma, and boil for 3 more minutes.

Step 5: Pop the funnel into your carboy, and pour in 3 gallons spring water.

Step 6: Stir your pot's contents, now known as the wort, into a good swirl, so the hops form a neat cone in the center. Then very carefully pour all the wort into the carboy, stopping before the hops pour out, too. Seal the carboy with a cap, and swirl vigorously until the water and wort are thoroughly mixed. If the carboy isn't filled up to where the neck narrows, top it off with more cold spring water and swirl again.

Step 7: Remove the cap, dip in your sterilized thermometer, and read the temp. If it's 78 degrees or cooler, sprinkle in the yeast. If it's warmer than 78 degrees, fill your tub or sink with cold water and a few ice cubes, and chill your carboy. (No double-dipping with your thermometer; sanitize it again before taking the next reading.)

Step 8: Once you've added the yeast, plug the carboy with your rubber stopper (the one with a hole in the middle) and slide in your plastic tubing (or fermentation hose). (Go easy, no need to jam it so far down that it touches your beer.) Put the other end of the hose into an old milk jug (or wine bottle, pot, or bucket, doesn't matter) filled a quarter of the way with water and a few drops of bleach. (It'll catch any runoff without allowing unsanitary air to blow back into the fermenter.)

Step 9: Chill out for 2 to 3 days and observe. During this time, your beer is going to bubble like crazy. It may even push some foam out the tube and into your runover jug. That's just the yeast, converting the malt's yummy sugars into alcohol and carbon dioxide.

Step 10: Once your beer stops bubbling, sanitize your fermentation lock. Then remove the hose and pop in the lock. Fill it with water, or even better, vodka. Air will be able to escape but bacteria won't be able to enter.

Step 11: Now, the hard part: waiting. Store your carboy in a dark, room-temperature place (like a closet), and let it sit for 2 weeks. Pass the time by dreaming up a name for your creation and, if you'd like, making bottle labels.

Step 12: Get ready to bottle your beer! First, wash and then sanitize your bottles, caps, plastic tubing (again), and 5-gallon plastic bucket by filling your tub with water, adding 1 tablespoon bleach for every gallon, and letting everything soak for 20 minutes. Rinse the bottles with boiling water, and then drain your bottles upside down on a drying rack.

Step 13: In a small pot, boil 2 cups water, add 5 ounces corn sugar (about ¾ cup), and stir until dissolved.

Step 14: Plunk your carboy on your countertop and remove the fermentation lock.

Step 15: Place the sanitized bucket on the floor below the carboy, and dump in the corn sugar mixture.

Step 16: Grab your hose, fill it with spring water, and cover the ends with your thumbs.

Step 17: Dunk one end of the hose into your beer and let the other end drain into the bucket. The rest of your beer will magically follow. Let all but the last ½ inch or so transfer to the bucket. This process, known as racking, helps separate your delicious beer from all the goopy sediment at the bottom.

Step 18: Plunk your beer-filled bucket on the countertop, and place your dry, sterilized bottles on the floor beneath it. Sterilize your tubing once more (for good measure), then fill it again with spring water, put your thumbs over the ends, dip one end into your beer and hold the other end below until your brew starts flowing.

Step 19: Put your hose into a bottle (all the way to the bottom), and fill to within an inch of the top. Pinch or bend the hose to stop the flow. Repeat, until all your bottles are full.

Step 20: Place your caps on each bottle (try not to touch their insides) and squeeze shut with your bottle-capper. If you've made labels, stick them on now.

Step 21: Store bottles at room temperature for 10 more days.

Step 22: Chill your home brew, and then drink up! Guaranteed, it'll be the best-tasting thing you've ever put to your lips.

More Nifty Tips

- If you don't want to buy beer bottles, ask a local bar to save their empties for you, or take a walk on recycling day.

- For other recipes, check the Web or ask your home brew supply store. Oftentimes, they'll sell ingredients in kits, based on the kind of beer (stout, lager, porter, etc.) you'd like to brew.

Toast to You

• • •

"My parents kept whiskey in the house. I grew up learning to have a little drink and learning how to handle it."
—Sue Westheimer Ransohoff

How to Mix the Perfect Cocktail

The Manhattan *(Very Dignified)*

Step 1: Fill your shiny silver cocktail shaker with ice. Begin salivating.

Step 2: Add 2 ounces bourbon.

Step 3: Add 1 ounce sweet vermouth.

Step 4: Add 5 to 6 dashes Angostura bitters.

Step 5: Stir vigorously, wiping drool from your chin with shirt-sleeve.

Step 6: Strain into a cocktail glass, and add a cherry, if you please.

Martini *(Very Froufrou!)*

Step 1: Pour 2 ounces gin over ice in a tall shaker.

Step 2: Add 1 ounce dry vermouth.

Step 3: Now for the secret, often overlooked, ingredient: Add a dash of orange bitters.

Step 4: Stir like crazy, until your shaker is sweating. (If you start sweating, too, then you know you're stirring *too* vigorously. Reel it in a bit.)

Step 5: Run a lemon twist around the edge of the glass.

Step 6: Pour your deliciousness into the glass through a strainer.

Step 7: Add your lemon twist by grasping both ends, gently turning hands in opposite directions until it spritzes into your cocktail. Then drop it in.

More Nifty Tips

- Sip your cocktails from small 2- to 3-ounce glasses, not giant fishbowls.

- Chill your glasses ahead of time by filling them with ice and water until you're ready to pour.

- Put on some music. Drinking while talking or dancing or singing is fun. Drinking in silence or while watching the boob tube is much less so.

Put Your Stamp on It

. . .

"We used to have parties at night every once in a while, and a fellow from out of town would bring his accordion. We had a big room, and we'd roll up the rugs and everybody would dance."
—Jean Dinsmore

How to Properly Extend an Invitation

Step 1: Plan your event. This one's a no-brainer, but before you invite any of your friends, you'll obviously need to figure out the date, location, and time of your party.

Step 2: Make a guest list. Consider the location of your fete. You don't want the space to be too crowded (sweaty!) or too empty (awkward!). Give your guest list a once-over to make sure you haven't missed anyone important to you. Then consider how your crew will mix and mingle, and make any necessary adjustments. You don't want to end up with, say, one single among a group of married couples, one man among a group of women, or one Fox newser among a group of MSNBCers.

Step 3: Choose your vibe. The invitation sets the tone of the entire event, so select one that best conveys the energy of the affair. Hands down, paper invitations, sent by mail, are always the most fun to receive. If it's a more casual affair, or you have less time to plan, e-mail or telephone invitations will do just fine.

Step 4: Two to three weeks before the party (or longer if it's a wedding or an event that requires travel), extend a personal invitation to each potential guest. (You may, of course, group couples and families together on one invitation.) Your goal is to make every possible attendee feel special, so don't lump everyone together in a mass e-mail; that's a quick way to make no one feel valued. Be sure to tell your invitees who is hosting the party, the location, the starting time, and, if you'd like, the ending time. Be prepared with directions, if necessary. And set a date by which you request their reply (regrets *and* acceptances). Usually a week's notice is enough to give you time to plan accordingly.

More Nifty Tips

- When making your guest list, figure about a 75 percent return rate.

- Unless it's a superformal affair, don't be shy about personalizing each invitation. Jot down a quick note, like, "I'd love to see you!" or "We miss you so much!" or "Hope you can come!"

Party On

. . .

"For a dinner party, the simpler the menu, the smoother the meal."
—GRACE FORTUNATO

HOW TO HOST A POTLUCK DINNER PARTY

Step 1: Make a guest list, based on the number of people (and seats) you can comfortably squeeze around your dining table (or your living room and kitchen, if it's a casual affair).

Step 2: Choose a general theme for the evening (e.g., Italian, Indian, Saint Patrick's Day, tropical). While you shouldn't dictate exactly what you'd like your guests to bring, a little guidance is often appreciated. Not only will it make it easier for your friends to choose a recipe, but it'll also help prevent any bad combos (e.g., sushi and fondue)—and bellyaches.

Step 3: Figure out how many dishes you'd like the meal to include. At minimum, you'll need an entrée (that's your job), a side, a salad, and a dessert. Appetizers and wine would be lovely, too.

Step 4: Extend a personal invitation to each of your guests, either in person or via telephone. Once you know whether they can attend, tell them the culinary theme of the meal and ask them to bring an appetizer, salad, side dish, or dessert. Any guests who are less handy in the kitchen (or pressed for time) can bring wine, bread, or a cheese plate. Be sure to check up front if anyone is vegetarian or has any food allergies.

Step 5: Before guests arrive, prepare the entrée, set the table, and clear any counter space (or oven space) necessary for their dishes. Set up a bar area, with ice, cups, corkscrews, and any beverages you're providing. Be prepared with any extra serving containers, ladles, tongs, or spatulas you might need to serve the feast. Turn on some tunes, plunk some flowers in a few vases, and light a few candles.

Step 6: When your pals arrive, give hugs and smooches, ask them what deliciousness they've brought and what, if any, further preparation is required. Then introduce them to your other friends and point them to the bar.

Step 7: Sit down, eat, drink, and be merry!

Step 8: Slip into the kitchen and wash your guests' dishes so you can return them at the evening's end. If you have any leftovers, offer them to the chef of the dish. Oftentimes, they'll let you keep them, but you shouldn't assume they're yours.

More Nifty Tips

- Keep a roll of masking tape and pen handy, and write the name of the owner on her respective dish, so you know whom to give what to.

- Though you may rely on your guests to bring wine, definitely keep a couple of bottles handy to get the party started. You never want your guests to go thirsty, especially if your wine-bringer is late. Also, some guests may not drink alcohol, so have some tasty bevies for them, too.

- If you plan on hosting three or fewer guests, prepare the evening's entrée and allow the others to bring only wine or dessert. Potlucks generally work best for larger groups, but feel rather stingy for smaller gatherings.

Make Connections

• • •

"When there are people here in my house, they're the
best people in the world."
—Sue Westheimer Ransohoff

How to Introduce People

Step 1: Figure out who has the higher rank or level of authority.
You've got all of a split second to make your choice, so don't dilly-
dally. Your boss, for example, trumps your buddy. Your lover trumps
your neighbor. If it's unclear, pick whoever is older.

Step 2: Name the more distinguished party, and present to her
the underparty. Include any relevant information she might like to
know. "Ms. President, may I present June Cleaver, my neighbor."
You can also substitute "have you met" for "may I present." On less
formal occasions, feel free to simply say both parties' names back-
to-back. "Laverne DeFazio, Shirley Feeney."

Step 3: You're finished! No need to do the reverse introduction
or repeat names. Your peeps already have all they need to know.

More Nifty Tips

• If you're introducing one person to a group, address the person
closest to you and present the newcomer to her. "Barb, this is
my colleague, Nicki." Then move around the group, simply
naming each of the members.

• Don't be bossy. Try to avoid making statements like "You must meet" or "Please shake hands with." No one likes being told what to do.

• If there's an awkward silence after you make the introduction, help your friends along by letting them know what they have in common, but keep it flattering. Rather than "Jo, have you met Blair? I think you both have hemorrhoids," say, "Jo, have you met Blair? You both went to the same boarding school."

Express Gratitude

...

"Sending a card is a gracious way of saying thank you and it makes people feel good. There is such a thing as doing something just to make people feel good."
—Ruth Rowen

HOW TO WRITE A THANK-YOU NOTE

Step 1: Find a nice card, or make one, and grab a pen. Thank-you cards should always be handwritten. It's more personal.

Step 2: Address the recipient by name: "Dear Matilda."

Step 3: Offer thanks for the gift, meal, helping hand, whatever. Begin the sentence with "Thank you for . . ." or "I'm so grateful for . . . ."

Step 4: State, in simple terms, why the gift or gesture touched you. (If it's a present you haven't put to use yet, say what you plan to do with it in the future.) Think, "Your pecan pie was so delicious. It was just what I needed after a hard day." Or "I plan to use the money to fulfill my lifelong dream of traveling to Paris this summer."

Step 5: Express your gratitude for the gift giver. After all, her presence in your life is more important than her presents in your life, right? Try something like, "You're always so thoughtful" or "I'm so grateful to have such a generous friend."

Step 6: Sign off. Try, "With love," "fondly," or "warmly," and then your name.

Step 7: Lick it, address it, stamp it, and send it!

More Nifty Tips

- Keep it short. A few heartfelt sentences will do.

- Don't get all highfalutin with your language. Write how you speak. Otherwise the receiver may suspect that the real you has been abducted by aliens.

- Be swift. The sooner you send your card, the more meaningful it will be.

Get a Laugh

• • •

*"We had parties. Your house was just open and people came. We'd sing
and dance and drink and sing more. It was really nice."*
—NIKKI SPANOF CHRISANTHON

HOW TO PLAY CHARADES

Step 1: Divide players into two equal teams of two or more, and
grab some paper, pencils, two hats (or bowls or baskets), a score pad,
and a stopwatch. Select a neutral timekeeper, or just take turns
minding the clock.

Step 2: Ask each player to write down a phrase on a slip of paper.
(If you have a bazillion people playing, teams can come up with,
say, five or so phrases collectively.) Once the phrases have been
chosen, fold the papers and toss them into your own team's hat. If
you'd like, you may agree, in advance, on certain categories, like famous people, songs, quotes, plays, movies, or books.

Step 3: Flip a coin (or thumb wrestle or, if it's that kind of party,
mud wrestle) to decide which team goes first, and then select one
person on the winning team to draw a phrase from the opposing
team's hat. Shh, keep it secret! Give that person a few seconds to
gather her thoughts, and then say "Go" and start the timer. Set a
have-mercy max of three minutes per round.

Step 4: Without making a peep, the lucky player must now act
out the chosen phrase until her teammates correctly guess it. (Aside

from letting out whelps of laughter, the other team should remain mum during this guessing phase.)

Step 5: If the team correctly shouts out the phrase, cheer and then jot down the amount of time it took them to do so. If their three minutes expire before they've gotten it, moan and jot down three minutes as their score. Take turns, alternating between teams and actors, until you've played all the slips of paper (or are too tired or too tipsy to proceed). The team with the lowest score wins.

More Nifty Tips

- When selecting phrases to write down, avoid total stumpers or long sentences, or your game will turn into a snoozefest.

- You don't have to act out each word in order. The best strategy is usually to convey the category of the phrase (a movie, a book, etc.), followed by the number of words in the phrase, the position of the word you're working on, the length of the word, and finally the syllables in that word. Start with the easiest word, and then go from there.

- Use these universal code gestures to indicate the category:

    A book: Put your hands together, as if in prayer but with fingers pointing outward, and then open them up.

    A movie: Pretend to operate an old-fashioned movie camera by forming an O with one hand in front of your eye (the lens) and cranking your other hand by your ear.

    A play: Get on bended knee, place one hand on your chest, and extend the other out to the side.

    A song: Pretend to sing.

    A TV show: Draw a square with two fingers.

    A quote: Make air quotes with your fingers.

A famous person: Do your best Napoleon. Puff up your chest and pretend to tuck one hand into the front of your shirt.

• Use these gestures to indicate the words:

The number of words in the phrase: Hold up the appropriate number of fingers.

The position of the word you're acting: Hold up the appropriate number of fingers once more.

The number of syllables in the word: Tap the appropriate number of fingers on your forearm.

The syllable you're acting: Tap the appropriate number of fingers on your forearm again.

The length of the word: Hold up your thumb and forefinger, spread small or large.

• Use these gestures to guide your team with their guessing:

A correct guess: Point to your nose with one hand, and the teammate who got it right with the other.

They're getting hot: Wipe sweat from your forehead.

They're getting cold: Wrap your arms around yourself and shiver.

Sounds like: Cup your hand behind your ear.

Plural: Link your pinkies.

Past tense: Wave your hand over your shoulder.

Raise Your Voice

. . .

*"We always sang around the piano. The best way to sing is in a group.
Stand next to someone who knows the part, and you'll be fine."*
—Lucile Frisbee

How to Sing in Harmony

Step 1: Round up one or more very forgiving, nonjudgmental
friends. Learning to sing in harmony takes a bit of practice, and you
will surely belt out some clunkers until you master it.

Step 2: Choose a simple song you'd like to sing that's in a major
key. (If it's a happy song, chances are it's in a major key. Sad songs
are often in minor keys.) The trickier the melody, the trickier the
harmony, so find a tune that requires only a small vocal range and no
scatting. "Row, Row, Row Your Boat" might be a good starter, since
the first three notes are the same.

Step 3: Master the melody. Sing together in unison until you nail
the right notes.

Step 4: Identify the root of your chord. Pick out the first note of
the melody on a pitch pipe, piano, or guitar, and say the name of the
note—A, B, C, D, E, F, or G—aloud.

Step 5: Find the third. Starting from the root, count up two notes
on the scale. So, if the root is a C, the third is an E. If it's an F, the
third is an A. If it's a G, the third is a B. And so on. Use your pitch

pipe (or piano or guitar) to play the third, take a deep breath, and let that note rip.

Step 6: Repeat steps 4 and 5 until you've picked out the harmony throughout the song. Or, if that's too much fuss, just choose several notes in the song to which you'd like to harmonize and sing the melody the rest of the time.

Step 7: Now, the fun part: Sing the song together from the beginning. On the pitch pipe (or whatever accompanying instrument you may be using), play the first note for the melody and then the harmony, find it with your voices, and begin.

Step 8: Keep practicing, and have fun! It'll get easier and more intuitive with every note you sing. You'll impress your friends in no time flat, so to speak.

More Nifty Tips

- Breathe deeply and sing with *oomph*. It's more difficult to harmonize if you hardly make a sound.

- You'll know you've hit the right note when you feel a blissful vibration. It's called resonance.

- To make a three-part harmony, find the root, and sing the third and fifth note on the scale. If the root is C, harmonize with an E and G.

- When in doubt, hold one finger in your ear. Not only will it help you hear what you're singing, but it'll also make you look like Mariah Carey. Cool!

Play Your Cards Right

• • •

"When I was growing up, we'd set up two or three tables, invite some people over, and play a different card game, like Old Maid or Crazy Eights, at each. You progressed from one table to the next. It was a neat get-together."
—ALICE LOFT

HOW TO PLAY CRAZY EIGHTS

Step 1: Deal seven cards to each player in a two-player game (or five cards in a three-or-more-player game), and place the remaining deck, facedown, in the center to form a stockpile. Flip over the top card and set it alongside.

Step 2: The person to the left of the dealer plays first. Let's assume that's you. You've got three options. (1) If you have a card in your hand that matches either the suit or rank (number or royalty) of the faceup card on the table, set it down, faceup, on top of that card. You're done! (2) If you have an eight, lucky you! Lay it down, and name the suit you'd like the next player to match. (3) If you have neither a matching card nor an eight, give a little moan and then draw from the stockpile until you select a card that you can play.

Step 3: Play proceeds clockwise. The first person to lay down all her cards wins!

More Nifty Tips

- Try to keep track of the cards already played, so when you play an eight, you can call the suit your neighbor will most likely *not* be holding.

- If you'd like to keep score, tally the cards that the losers are left holding at the end of each round. Each numbered card is worth face value, except eights; they're worth 50. Aces are 1 and face cards are 10. All points are awarded to the winner of that round. A two-player game ends when the winner reaches 100, a three-player game ends when the winner reaches 150, and so on.

You Might as Well Dance

• • •

"To be a good dancer, you just have to like to dance."
—Lucile Frisbee

How to Do a Basic Waltz

Step 1: Place your right hand in your partner's left hand and your left hand on his shoulder, keeping your elbows pointed out and upper arms parallel to the floor. Start counting (inside your head and, here's the tough part, without moving your lips, if you can help it) 1-2-3, 1-2-3, 1-2-3. Start in super slow motion until you get it down.

Step 2: On the one-count, step your right foot back about a foot, landing toe-heel.

Step 3: On the two-count, step your left foot back and to the left, landing only on your toe.

Step 4: On the three-count, slide your right foot to your left, landing first on your toe, and then setting both heels down.

Step 5: Start your count again. On the one-count, step your left foot forward about a foot, landing heel-toe.

Step 6: On the two-count, step your right foot forward and to right, landing only on your toe.

Step 7: On the three-count, slide your left foot to your right, landing first on your toe, and then setting both heels down. Repeat the sequence until the music stops or your dogs start barking.

More Nifty Tips

- Stand tall, throw your shoulders back, and try to look into your partner's eyes, not at your tootsies.

- To help you remember the motions, you can ditch the numbers ("1, 2, 3") and think instead, "Back, side, together. Forward, side, together."

- Don't worry if you step on a few toes or bump into other people. Just get out on the dance floor, or makeshift dance floor, and have fun. If you're happy and having a good time, nothing else matters.

Acknowledgments
. . .

I had so much help writing this book, so here is a huge, heartfelt thank-you:

To all of the special grandmothers who shared their stories and wisdom with me. I feel honored to know you. Especially Elouise Bruce of Cleveland, Mississippi, who showed me that the richness of your life has nothing to do with your bank statement; Nikki Spanof Chrisanthon, who is one of the best dancers I know; Jean Dinsmore of Spokane, Washington, who reminded me of the pleasure of home-baked bread; Grace Fortunato, who showed me that life is about love, not stuff; Lucile Frisbee of Delhi, New York, who invited me into her home, served me tea in china cups, and sent me off with a jug of her own maple syrup; Mildred Kalish of Cupertino, California, who inspired me with her book and shared her secret to making a juicy roasted chicken; Alice Loft of Tacoma, Washington, who taught me how to build a fire and warmed my heart; Beatrice Neidorf of Washington, D.C., who reminded me that pie crusts are nothing to fear; Sue Westheimer Ransohoff of Cincinnati, Ohio, who taught me about the value of being generous; and Ruth Rowen, who welcomed me into her home to share stories—and chocolate cupcakes. Thank you.

To my wonderful editor, Jill Schwartzman. You rock! And to all my new friends at Random House, including Jane von Mehren, Kim Hovey, Anne Watters, Kathleen McAuliffe, Theresa Zoro, Katie Rudkin, Rachel Bernstein, and Lea Beresford. Thanks for all your hard work and good ideas.

To all the modern-day experts in my neighborhood and beyond, who offered their guidance on some of the more technical tips. Especially Chef Karen Bornarth, bread instructor at the French Culinary Institute in New York, New York; designers Patti Gilstrap and Seryn Potter, owners of Flirt Brooklyn and Home Ec sewing school in Brooklyn; Chef Juventino Avila, owner of Get Fresh Table and Market in Brooklyn; brewer Shane C. Welch, owner of Sixpoint Craft Ales in Brooklyn; knifemaker Joel Bukiewicz, owner of Cut Brooklyn; money whiz Jonathan F. Walsh, a certified public accountant in New York, New York; farmer Benjamin Shute, co-owner of Hearty Roots Community Farm in Tivoli, New York; music teacher Alicia Mathewson of the Sounding Still Center of Love in Barnstable, Massachusetts; and winemakers Don and Rosalind Heinert, owners of Blueberry Sky Farm Winery in North East, Pennsylvania.

To Lucy Danziger and all my friends at *SELF*, for creating a magazine I'm proud of.

To my parents, Bill and Claire, who taught me how to tie ties and bake pies, and my in-laws, Norm and Shirley, who taught me how to catch a fish and fry it up.

To Holly Bemiss, my literary agent and angel, for believing in me, supporting me, and making every single day of my life better.

ABOUT THE AUTHOR

ERIN BRIED is a senior staff writer at *SELF* magazine. She lives with her better half in Brooklyn, New York, where she grows tomatoes on her fire escape, knits crooked scarves for loved ones, and eats homemade pie for breakfast as often as possible.